KEI

LILREKA SMITH

COMFORT ZONERS
-VS-
OWNERS

Truthfully, Which One Are You?

Author Keith Smith
P.O. Box 1792
Bridgeview, IL 60455

Comfort Zoners -vs- Owners: Truthfully, Which One Are You?

ISBN 978-1727137972

ARD Book Services
Book Consultant/Publisher
www.ardbookservices.com
345 Laverne Avenue, # Suite 14
Hillside, Illinois 60162

ARD
Book Services

To make a payment or if you would like to give a donation, it will be greatly appreciated. Please feel free to:

Cash App $KeithSmithOwner

QuickPay or Zelle @ keithsmithowner@gmail.com

I THANK YOU IN ADVANCE FOR YOUR SUPPORT!!!

DEDICATION

This Book is dedicated to You! Yes you, the one who is reading this book right now. This is your BOOK to keep for a Lifetime. You are GREATER than Anything and Anyone that's trying to Stop you from Improving in your Life. Believe in yourself, No one can stop you But you, Right? Forgive yourself and move on. Enjoy your Book and Make today a Great day for Yourself, It's Possible!

COMFORT ZONER overall Meaning: A person who wants to change for the better BUT does not want to be a part of his/her change to become better.

OWNER overall Meaning: A person who takes ownership and owns up to their responsibilities in order to create the necessary change in their life.

"DESTROY YOUR COMFORT ZONE
TO BECOME A BETTER YOU"
IT'S POSSIBLE!

CAN YOU PLEASE HELP ME?

Can you please help me with one thing and one thing only? To reach over one hundred million people to let them know that We AGREE with them that they are GREATER than their Comfort Zone. By taking a picture with you and your book, post the picture on Facebook or Instagram tag/add me to your post. I can't reach this many people by myself. I really need your help and support to spread the message throughout this book Comfort Zoners -vs- Owners. Please write the message listed below as the caption. Thank you for your help and support.

Caption-I AGREE WITH YOU! "You are GREATER than Your Comfort Zone". This Book is available for you on Amazon.

Facebook: Keith Smith Owner

Instagram: @keithsmithowner

Available on Amazon.com

Sincerely,
Keith Smith

THANK YOU

My wife Lilreka Smith and I would like to thank you for taking the time to buy, read and evaluate yourself through this transformable book. We hope and pray that you will continue to not just be busy in life BUT you will be productive in whatever you do and prosper even as your soul prosper.

SETTING THE ATMOSPHERE SPEECH

Hey listen up! I am not here to hear. I repeat, I am not here to hear. I repeat, I am not here to hear the critics and negative people that appear and after I finish talking they quickly disappear, but I am here to talk to those with a listening ear. So can I get your attention for the people that are here and want to hear and be transformed through the power of words with no trace of fear, no trace of fear, no trace of fear? This is live, so if I make a mistake…it's called life. I'm sure we can all agree that in life we make mistakes right? What we must understand is that mistakes are only proof that we are trying. If you are not trying to IMPROVE yourself, then I am not trying to be around YOU.

By Keith Smith

MY MISSION

To spread the message throughout this book to help over 100 million people acknowledge their COMFORT ZONE, and to show you how to transform your mind in order to destroy your comfort zone DAILY. To become a better you.
It's possible!

By Keith Smith

CONTENTS

PART ONE: MENTALLY

1. POEM! Comfort Zoners vs Owners 19
2. Success! 20
3. Impossible!...21
4. New Year's Resolution!..22
5. Tomorrow! 23
6. To Do List! 23
7. Keep!...24
8. Else! 25
9. Social Media! 25
10. Habits!...26
11. Mindset! 27
12. Hope! 28
13. It Takes Time!...28
14. Life! 29
15. Beginning! 29
16. Say! 30
17. If! 31
18. Presidential Elections! 32
19. Same Place Different Strategies! 33
20. You Still Waiting? 34
21. Who's In Your Circle? 35
22. Wealthy Person!..36
23. Imagination!..36
24. Work For!...37

25. Building! 38

26. What's Happening? 38

27. Suggest! 39

28. Authority! 40

29. Places! 40

30. Familiar! 41

31. Thoughts! 42

32. Stop Searching! 42

33. Look At! 43

34. Valuable! 44

35. Support! 44

36. See! 45

37. Rush! 46

38. Leads! 46

39. Multiple! 47

40. Obstacles! 47

41. Wear! 48

42. Change! 49

43. You Can't Deceive Me! (A Short Story) 50

PART TWO: SPIRITUALLY

44. Thank God! 57

45. Cleanliness! 57

46. Told! 58

47. Progress! 59

48. Pray! 60

49. Forgive and Apologize! 61

50. Desire! 62

51. God is Faithful! 62

52. Doctor! 63

53. Kill! 64

54. What God Wants! 65
55. Heal! 66
56. Promote! 67
57. Make It! 67
58. Devil! 68
59. According! 69
60. Doubt! 69
61. Bible! 70
62. Choose! 70
63. Mailbox! 71
64. Knowledge! 71
65. Expect! 72
66. Pray For! 73
67. Encourage! 74
68. Leadership! 74
69. Them! 75
70. People! 76
71. I Want To Be Just Like Him! (A Short Story) 76

PART THREE: PHYSICALLY

72. I Fired My Boss! 83
73. Key! 84
74. States! 85
75. 15 Years! 85
76. Picture! 86
77. Clock! 87
78. Dedicated! 87
79. Vision! 88
80. Step Out! 89
81. Retire! 89

82. When Times Get Hard! 90

83. Connected! 91

84. Chores List! 92

85. Accomplish! 95

86. Routine! 95

87. Own! 98

88. Goal! 98

89. Paid! 99

90. Fake Smile! 100

91. Environment! 100

92. Proof! 101

93. What You Want To Do? 102

94. Believe! 103

95. Busy! 103

96. Perfect! 104

97. Dream! 105

98. Old Self! 105

99. No Call, No Show! 106

100. Maintain! 107

101. Struggles! 107

102. House! 108

103. Motivate! 109

104. Call! 109

105. Excuse! 110

106. Wake Up! 110

107. Light! 111

108. Committed! 112

109. Promotion! 112

110. Hard! 113

111. Parent Teacher Conference! 114

112. Busy -vs- Productive! 115

113. Tried!..116

114. Respect!..117

115. Started!..118

116. Foolishness! 118

117. Build! 119

118. Given! 120

119. Show Up!..120

120. Something!..121

121. Events! 121

122. Sundays!..122

123. Trip! 123

124. Degree!..123

125. Best! 124

126. Into!..125

127. Time!...125

128. Please! 126

129. Bed!..127

130. Slaves/Masters! 127

131. Garbage!..128

132. Laid off! 129

133. Watch!...130

134. Process!...130

135. Nothing! 131

136. Apply! 131

137. Project!..132

138. Like! (True Story) 133

PART FOUR: FINANCIALLY

139. Two Guys! 139

140. Shoulders! 139

141. Money, Money, Money! 140

142. Say! 141

143. Income Tax Money!.............................142

144. Charge!..143

145. Enough!...144

146. Allergic! 145

147. Monday! 145

148. Unemployment! 146

149. Spending Money!..............................147

150. Raise! 148

151. Business! 148

152. Die!..149

153. Look! (True Story) 150

PART FIVE: EMOTIONALLY

154. Acknowledge! 157

155. No! 157

156. With! 158

157. Based On!..159

158. It's Ok!..160

159. Something! 160

160. Self Help! 161

161. Look Down! 162

162. Hourly Pay! 163

163. Write Ups!..164

164. I Am Out Of Here!.............................165

165. Restroom!...165

166. Critics!...166

167. Cry! 167

168. Reject! 168

169. How You Doing!................................168

170. Ask!...169

171. Stress-Free! 170

172. Gossip! 170

173. Energy! 171

174. Debates! 172

175. Point! 173

176. Quick! 173

177. Working! 174

178. Uplift! 174

179. Inside! 175

180. Children! 176

181. Years Ago! 176

182. Themselves! 177

183. Hurt! 178

184. I Became! (A Short Story) 179

185. Yes/No! 196

186. Your Vision! 196

187. Stop Expecting People To! 197

PART 1

MENTALLY

COMFORT ZONER overall meaning: A person who wants to change for the better BUT does not want to be a part of his/her change to become better.

OWNER overall meaning: A person who takes ownership and owns up to their responsibilities in order to create the necessary change in their life.

My Wife & I Agree With You!

"You are GREATER than Anything and Anyone who tries to Stop you from Improving your Life. Believe in yourself, No one can stop you but you. Right? Forgive yourself and move on. Make Today a Great day for Yourself. It's Possible!"

By Keith Smith

POEM!

"Comfort Zoner -vs- Owner"

Hey listen up. Would you agree, that there's no one who can stop you but you? Would you agree, that you are GREATER than Anything and Anyone that will try to stop you from improving in your LIFE? Well let me tell you about two different people. One called a comfort zoner and the other called an owner. I am not here to hurt you, but I am here to tell you about ownership. Would you agree, that people say that they own their house? Would you agree, that people say that they own their spouse? Would you agree, that people say that they own their car? Well let's break something down and you choose which one you are. Can we really be honest with ourselves? A lot of things you said you own, you really don't own, because if you are a comfort zoner, you are three write ups and three paychecks away from losing your car and your home. You say you own your spouse but that's a lie too, because if you understood that ownership is about creating something not simply what is next to you. A comfort zoner is a person that wants to change for the better, but complains about what they have and where they work and are not willing to be a part of their change to become better. A comfort zoner, is a person that works a job from 9 to 5.

The owner is the one that owns the clock you punch in and out of and also owns your lives. A comfort zoner says things like, "I can go where I want and do what I choose." That is a lie because they have to make sure they get permission from the owner to be excused. Owners are the people that create the plan and then hire the comfort zoner to work hard to maintain their plan. So I say, do not just work hard and maintain the owner's plan, but be apart and start owning something in this land. Which one will you become? A owner or a comfort zoner? You choose but just remember if you do not own anything and do not create anything, the owner wins and you lose. Start creating and controlling your freedom and your peace of mind. Own something and continue owning over time.

Truthfully! really truthfully, Which One Are You? Because the only person who can seriously answer this question truthfully, is YOU.

□ Comfort Zoner
□ Owner

Tip: Stop looking for excuses, people and things to blame, just except your past and create your change. It's possible!
Let's Connect @KeithSmithOwner

# SUCCESS!

COMFORT ZONERS: Think success is having a lot of money, a lot of materialistic things and owning a profitable business only.

OWNERS: Know success comes in many forms such as, success in your peace of mind, which is mental. Success in your body, which is physical. Success in your feelings, which is emotional. Success in your wealth, which is financial. Success in your faith, which is spiritual and success in loving and taking care of your family, which is unity. They understand that those are truly the balance of being successful.

Truthfully! really truthfully, Which One Are You? Because the only person who can seriously answer this question truthfully, is YOU.

PART 1: MENTALLY

□ Comfort Zoner
□ Owner

Tip: Work towards becoming a successful owner in Every Area of your Life, it's possible. Let's Connect @KeithSmithOwner

MPOSSIBLE!

COMFORT ZONERS: Look at "impossible" as a stop sign, fear, doubt, it must not be for me. I cannot do it, it is too hard. I am tired. It is not possible. I quit, it will not work out. I am going to fail at doing it. I have tried, I am done, I do not know how and etc.

OWNERS: Turn their "impossible" to make it "I am possible" to create it to become "possible". Owners say if I fail at trying, I am going to keep going forward towards completing what I have started until I get it right.

Truthfully! really truthfully, Which One Are You? Because the only person who can seriously answer this question truthfully, is YOU.

□ Comfort Zoner
□ Owner

Tip: Nothing or no one can stop you but you, it's possible. Let's Connect @KeithSmithOwner

NEW YEAR'S

RESOLUTION!

COMFORT ZONERS: Are the people that make new year resolutions without a strategy or plan put in place in order to complete their New Year's resolution. They simply say things such as, "I am going to lose weight this year, get a house this year, forgive somebody this year, get out of debt this year" and etc. their plan is only I believe that I will receive without putting an action in place. They make the same New Year resolutions every year and never complete them.

OWNERS: Are the people that make a new year resolution, but they create a strategic plan and take action to accomplish their resolution. They say things such as, "I am going to lose weight this year, create another company this year, get out of debt this year, get a new house this year" and etc. They create a plan detailing when, where, why, how and what they are going to do to complete their plan for the year. They start working towards it and accomplish it. They make New Year's resolution plans every year and completed them.

Truthfully! really truthfully, Which One Are You? Because the only person who can seriously answer this question truthfully, is YOU.

☐ Comfort Zoner
☐ Owner

Tip: Plan, strategize and execute your plan until you complete it. It's possible. Let's Connect @KeithSmithOwner

TOMORROW!

COMFORT ZONERS: Put off what they can do today until tomorrow.

OWNERS: Do what they can do today, so they can work and focus on something new for tomorrow.

Truthfully! really truthfully, Which One Are You? Because the only person who can seriously answer this question truthfully, is YOU.

☐ Comfort Zoner
☐ Owner

Tip: Tomorrow is not promise, do it TODAY, it's possible. Let's Connect @KeithSmithOwner

TO DO LIST!

COMFORT ZONERS: Do not write out a to do list daily.

OWNERS: Write out a to do list daily because they understand that minds forget but notes do not. They also understand that writing out a to do list daily helps them keep their word and promises made with someone else. To do list's also help them stay clutter free and organized. Owners understand when making a to do list daily they can get more done in a day because they are prioritizing and taking control of their day. Instead of their day taking control of them.

Truthfully! really truthfully, Which One Are You? Because the only person who can seriously answer this question truthfully, is YOU.

☐ Comfort Zoner
☐ Owner

Tip: Create a To-Do-List daily, it's possible. Let's Connect @KeithSmithOwner

 **K**EEP!

COMFORT ZONERS: Focus and keep their mind on things they do not desire.

OWNERS: Focus and keep their mind on things they desire.

Truthfully! really truthfully, Which One Are You? Because the only person who can seriously answer this question truthfully, is YOU.

☐ Comfort Zoner
☐ Owner

Tip: Focus on what you really desire to accomplish in your life, it's possible. Let's Connect @KeithSmithOwner

PART 1: MENTALLY

ELSE!

COMFORT ZONERS: Believe in everything and everyone else BUT themselves.

OWNERS: Believe in themselves, so they can make everything that they believe in that is invisible become visible. For an owner everything that seems impossible becomes possible.

Truthfully! really truthfully, Which One Are You? Because the only person who can seriously answer this question truthfully, is YOU.

☐ Comfort Zoner
☐ Owner

Tip: Have Confidence in and about yourself, it's possible. Let's Connect @KeithSmithOwner

SOCIAL MEDIA!

COMFORT ZONERS: Stay on social media all day and expect to change or expect something great to happen for them. They waste time complaining about their homework, test scores, class grade, job, their pay, their house and want to change things but they are on social media all day and do not understand that the power of accepting change starts with them first.

OWNERS: Understand the importance of stepping away from social media, so they can be productive and able to use their brain

Destroy your Comfort Zone, or it will destroy you!

to brainstorm and create something great. Unless they are using social media to promote or create something great, other than that, owners couldn't care less about being on social media.

Truthfully! really truthfully, Which One Are You? Because the only person who can seriously answer this question truthfully, is YOU.

□ Comfort Zoner
□ Owner

Tip: Use Social Media in Moderation, it's possible. Let's Connect @KeithSmithOwner

 # Habits!

COMFORT ZONERS: Build habits to where they do not want to go and be at in their life. Habits such as procrastination, doubt, fear, lying, cheating, stealing and etc.

OWNERS: Build habits to where they want to go and be at in their life. Owners understand everyone is where they are in their life today because of the habits they made and built yesterday.

Truthfully! really truthfully, Which One Are You? Because the only person who can seriously answer this question truthfully, is YOU.

□ Comfort Zoner
□ Owner

Tip: Start creating positive daily habits, it's possible. Let's Connect @KeithSmithOwner

 Mindset!

COMFORT ZONERS: Have a defeated mindset. They say and think I cannot do that, they do not like me, they are racist, I can never get ahead, I am always late on paying something, I might lose if I give my service away for free sometimes, they might tell me no if I ask them, and etc.

OWNERS: Have an overcoming, conquering and winning mindset. They take faith action, they know they can do and create whatever they are working on, they always get ahead in whatever they do. They give their service away for free sometimes because that brings growth and expansion to their company and they win. They turn "Impossible" to "I'm Possible" to create it to become possible. They have a growth mindset.

Truthfully! really truthfully, Which One Are You? Because the only person who can seriously answer this question truthfully, is YOU.

☐ Comfort Zoner
☐ Owner

Tip: Get rid of your excuses and defeated thinking so you can start to grow and expand, it's possible. Let's Connect
@KeithSmithOwner

12 HOPE!

COMFORT ZONERS: Say things like "just hope for the best but expect the worst."

OWNERS: Hope for and create the best.

Truthfully! really truthfully, Which One Are You? Because the only person who can seriously answer this question truthfully, is YOU.

☐ Comfort Zoner
☐ Owner

> **Tip:** Stop expecting what you do not want to have or happen in your life, it's possible. Let's Connect
> @KeithSmithOwner

13 IT TAKES TIME!

If you only hope and look for the person you want to be, you will need to look for the rest of your earthly life. If you create the person you want to be, it will only take change, patience, time and process to become that person you want to become. It is possible! Keep moving forward and upward.

Choose One:
☐ Agree
☐ Disagree

LIFE!

COMFORT ZONERS: Think life is about finding yourself.

OWNERS: Know life is about creating the person you want to become.

Truthfully! really truthfully, Which One Are You? Because the only person who can seriously answer this question truthfully, is YOU.

☐ Comfort Zoner
☐ Owner

BEGINNING!

COMFORT ZONERS: Think that their beginning is the end. So they are scared to create and own something. They say things like, "I might fail at being an owner, what if it does not turn out right, everybody is not made to be an owner and etc. So I will just stay right here in my comfort zone and keep hoping something great happens to me."

Destroy your Comfort Zone, or it will destroy you!

OWNERS: Understand that their end shall be better than their beginning. That is why they go through life owning and creating things with no sweat. They say, "I am going to make this work out no matter how hard this is. If I fail while creating and owning, that just shows that I am continuing to pursue what I am creating and learning from it until I get it right. I am creating the impossible into possible."

Truthfully! really truthfully, Which One Are You? Because the only person who can seriously answer this question truthfully, is YOU.

□ Comfort Zoner
□ Owner

Tip: Stop being afraid to take a step to create and own something. Just step out, it's possible. Let's Connect
@KeithSmithOwner

 **16 SAY!**

COMFORT ZONERS: Will say stop bragging before you lose it all. See they have a "losing it all" mentality before even receiving something.

OWNERS: Say keep being thankful and keep grinding so you can get more. See they have a growth mentality and receiving all they go out and get without doubting themselves before making a move.

Truthfully! really truthfully, Which One Are You? Because the only person who can seriously answer this question truthfully, is YOU.

PART 1: MENTALLY

☐ Comfort Zoner
☐ Owner

Tip: Replace your losing it all mentality with a gaining mentality so you can grow in your life. It's possible. Let's Connect @KeithSmithOwner

IF!

COMFORT ZONERS: Have a business mindset. If something does not work out for them or it gets too hard they will turn back and return to punch in at an owner's work clock. They say things like "I need company benefits" for themselves and their children.

OWNERS: Have an owner's mindset. If something is not working out or gets too hard for an owner they keep pushing forward and upward until things work out. They never look and go back. They overcome every obstacle that comes their way. They create company benefits for themselves, their children and the comfort zoners who work for them.

Truthfully! really truthfully, Which One Are You? Because the only person who can seriously answer this question truthfully, is YOU.

☐ Comfort Zoner
☐ Owner

Tip: You were born to dominate and overcome any fear and obstacles that gets in your way. It's possible. Let's Connect @KeithSmithOwner

Destroy your Comfort Zone, or it will destroy you!

PRESIDENTIAL

ELECTIONS!

While the elections are going on as an owner they continue creating because one thing they realize is no matter who is in the white house, they have to work out their own creativity, responsibilities and situations in their life. If an owner focuses on what president is going to be elected it can cause them to get off course and lose focus on what they are supposed to be creating. While everyone else is concerned about what one man is going to do for them and to them, and forget to do anything for themselves. It isn't going to benefit them anyway no matter who is elected.

Owners do not fill their mind with the presidential election. They just pray for whoever wins the presidential elections. They fill their minds with creating something for the next generation that comes up after them to be a part of their creation. Owners do not tell you to vote or not to vote, that is your choice.

Should you Vote?
□ Yes
□ No

Tip: Focus on what you are supposed to be focusing on, it's important and remember it's possible. Let's Connect @KeithSmithOwner

 SAME PLACE DIFFERENT STRATEGIES!

COMFORT ZONERS: Say I am at Starbucks playing chess not checkers. A checkers player looks to take the man down next to them right away, while chess players move strategically to move the king out the way! Long term moves.

OWNERS: Say I am at Starbucks creating another chess board game so others can play to move the kings out the way. Long term creating. Owners create it, comfort zoners buy and play it. Owners say, "while you play it, I will continuously make money from it. So now who is really the king?"

Truthfully! really truthfully, Which One Are You? Because the only person who can seriously answer this question truthfully, is YOU.

☐ Comfort Zoner
☐ Owner

Tip: Create the Plan and deploy it, it's possible. Let's Connect @KeithSmithOwner

Destroy your Comfort Zone, or it will destroy you!

YOU STILL WAITING?

COMFORT ZONERS: Wait and want everything to come to them. They want to get paid for doing nothing but sitting around and procrastinating all day.

OWNERS: They go out and create what they want to have in their lives.

Truthfully! really truthfully, Which One Are You? Because the only person who can seriously answer this question truthfully, is YOU.

☐ Comfort Zoner
☐ Owner

Tip: Go out and create what you need. Keyword GO, it's possible. Let's Connect @KeithSmithOwner

WHO'S IN

YOUR CIRCLE?

COMFORT ZONERS: Will try to keep you in their box or in their circle. They will have you talking their "fear of change" language, living there no growth lifestyle, working where they work. They want you around the same people they associate with so that you can stay in the same comfort zone mentality that they are in. When they keep you on their no growth level it makes them feel powerful instead of powerless.

OWNERS: They surround themselves with people who are growing and expanding. People who are going to challenge them to grow and think outside the box.

Truthfully! really truthfully, Which One Are You? Because the only person who can seriously answer this question truthfully, is YOU.

☐ Comfort Zoner
☐ Owner

Tip: Surround yourself around owners and create like an owner. Get away from comfort zone type of people quickly! Delete their numbers, social media, friend request and steer them out of your life before you pick up their comfort zone habits. It's possible! Let's Connect @KeithSmithOwner

Destroy your Comfort Zone, or it will destroy you!

WEALTHY

PERSON!

COMFORT ZONERS: Get excited about talking to or seeing a wealthy person. They say things such as, "there he/she is right there, I cannot believe who I am seeing right now or let me try to get an autograph or picture with them."

OWNERS: Get excited about becoming a wealthy person. They say things such as, "wow! Look what I have become."

Truthfully! really truthfully, Which One Are You? Because the only person who can seriously answer this question truthfully, is YOU.

☐ Comfort Zoner
☐ Owner

Tip: Become what you are excited about seeing, it's possible.
Let's Connect @KeithSmithOwner

IMAGINATION!

COMFORT ZONERS: Build up obstacles of defeat in their imagination to stop them before even getting started, moving forward and creating something.

OWNERS: Get rid of and cast down obstacles out of their imaginations as soon as they come.

Truthfully! really truthfully, Which One Are You? Because the only person who can seriously answer this question truthfully, is YOU.

☐ Comfort Zoner
☐ Owner

> **Tip:** Replace your negative thoughts with positive thoughts quickly so you can move forward in your life. It's possible!
> Let's Connect @KeithSmithOwner

 **W**ORK **F**OR!

COMFORT ZONERS: Say, "I do not know how to own my own. That is why I choose to work for someone else."

OWNERS: Say, "I have chosen to learn how to create and own my own, so I do not have to work for someone else."

Truthfully! really truthfully, Which One Are You? Because the only person who can seriously answer this question truthfully, is YOU.

☐ Comfort Zoner
☐ Owner

> **Tip:** Learn how to create and own your own, it's possible.
> Let's Connect @KeithSmithOwner

Destroy your Comfort Zone, or it will destroy you!

25 BUILDING!

COMFORT ZONERS: Talk and gossip to each other about what the owner is creating and building.

OWNERS: Keep creating and building while the comfort zoner talks and gossips about them. They say, "you are talking about me now but you will be working and punching my work clock later".

Truthfully! really truthfully, Which One Are You? Because the only person who can seriously answer this question truthfully, is YOU.

☐ Comfort Zoner
☐ Owner

Tip: Use your thoughts and voice to create something positive instead of gossiping about something negative. It's possible!
Let's Connect @KeithSmithOwner

26 WHAT'S

HAPPENING?

COMFORT ZONERS: Can tell you what event is going to happen, but they cannot give you full details. They say things like, "I am only telling you what I know so far, until I get more information from my boss."

OWNERS: Can tell you when the event is going to happen. Where it is going to happen. The reason or occasion. Why it is happening. Who the event is for and how it is happening. Simply because they created the event.

Truthfully! really truthfully, Which One Are You? Because the only person who can seriously answer this question truthfully, is YOU.

☐ Comfort Zoner
☐ Owner

Tip: Become that person who creates events to happen, it's possible. Let's Connect @KeithSmithOwner

UGGEST!

COMFORT ZONERS: Will speak and suggest something and then wait for everyone else to give an opinion.

OWNERS: Speak or make suggestions then change and transformations happen instantly.

Truthfully! really truthfully, Which One Are You? Because the only person who can seriously answer this question truthfully, is YOU.

☐ Comfort Zoner
☐ Owner

Tip: Speak to make negative situations become drastically

eradicated and transformed, it's possible. Let's Connect
@KeithSmithOwner

28 AUTHORITY!

COMFORT ZONERS: Ask, expect and demand respect and authority.

OWNERS: Put in the work for respect and authority. They understand respect and authority does not just happen, it starts with self-respect first.

Truthfully! really truthfully, Which One Are You? Because the only person who can seriously answer this question truthfully, is YOU.

☐ Comfort Zoner
☐ Owner

Tip: Give respect to receive respect, it's possible. Let's Connect
@KeithSmithOwner

29 PLACES!

COMFORT ZONERS: Are scared to go places others will not go.

OWNERS: Go places where others will not go. That is why they constantly grow and expand. They are not scared to take a risk. They get comfortable with being uncomfortable.

Truthfully! really truthfully, Which One Are You? Because the only person who can seriously answer this question truthfully, is YOU.

☐ Comfort Zoner
☐ Owner

Tip: Do the positive things that others is scared to do, it's possible. Let's Connect @KeithSmithOwner

30 **F**AMILIAR!

COMFORT ZONERS: Cannot grow because they are scared to leave everything that they are familiar with.

OWNERS: Grow because they leave everything that they are familiar with and venture out to create change and expand.

Truthfully! really truthfully, Which One Are You? Because the only person who can seriously answer this question truthfully, is YOU.

☐ Comfort Zoner
☐ Owner

Tip: Do something positive that you have never done before. Go somewhere positive where you have never gone before, it's possible. Let's Connect @KeithSmithOwner

31 THOUGHTS!

COMFORT ZONERS: Just go with any thought that they are thinking.

OWNERS: Evaluate the thoughts that come to their mind.

Truthfully! really truthfully, Which One Are You? Because the only person who can seriously answer this question truthfully, is YOU.

☐ Comfort Zoner
☐ Owner

> **Tip:** Take a thought before taking action on anything. In other words think before acting, it's possible. Let's Connect @KeithSmithOwner

32 STOP

SEARCHING!

COMFORT ZONERS: Search for growth and expansion outside of themselves.

OWNERS: Understand that everything they need is inside of them. That as long as they stay obedient to God, the vision and purpose inside of them will be created and pushed out.

Truthfully! really truthfully, Which One Are You? Because the only person who can seriously answer this question truthfully, is YOU.

☐ Comfort Zoner
☐ Owner

Tip: Everything you will ever need is on the inside of you. Focus, work and create it to come out of you. Only you have the power to do that, it's possible. Let's Connect @KeithSmithOwner

⭐ LOOK AT!

COMFORT ZONERS: Look at an obstacle and let it stop them from creating and going forth in life.

OWNERS: Look at an obstacle and use that obstacle to push them to another level in life.

Truthfully! really truthfully, Which One Are You? Because the only person who can seriously answer this question truthfully, is YOU.

☐ Comfort Zoner
☐ Owner

Tip: You were born to dominate and overcome stress, obstacles and pain, it's possible. Let's Connect @KeithSmithOwner

Destroy your Comfort Zone, or it will destroy you!

34 VALUABLE!

COMFORT ZONERS: Think that materialistic things are more valuable than them. Such as vehicles, homes, vacations, degrees, clothes etc.

OWNERS: Understand that they are more valuable than materialistic things because they are the people who are creating and not being controlled by them.

Truthfully! really truthfully, Which One Are You? Because the only person who can seriously answer this question truthfully, is YOU.

☐ Comfort Zoner
☐ Owner

Tip: Create and control the substance do not let the substance control and Create you, it's possible. Let's Connect @KeithSmithOwner

35 SUPPORT!

COMFORT ZONERS: Expect only the people they know to support them in what they are doing. With that mindset they have stopped their growth already before they even begin to grow.

OWNERS: Expect the people they know and do not know to support them in what they are doing. That is why they continue to expand and grow in their life.

Truthfully! really truthfully, Which One Are You? Because the only person who can seriously answer this question truthfully, is YOU.

☐ Comfort Zoner
☐ Owner

Tip: Get the right people to help your vision to grow and not just the people you know, it's possible. Let's Connect @KeithSmithOwner

36 SEE!

COMFORT ZONERS: See themselves in bondage, self-pity, overtaken, defeated, neglected, low self-esteem, guilty and many more.

OWNERS: See themselves as creators, royalty, kings and queens, obstacle defeaters, problem solvers, stress defeaters, builders, encouragers, counselors and many more.

Truthfully! really truthfully, Which One Are You? Because the only person who can seriously answer this question truthfully, is YOU.

☐ Comfort Zoner
☐ Owner

Tip: You are born to overcome every negative thought and circumstance that comes into your life. It's possible. Let's Connect @KeithSmithOwner

Destroy your Comfort Zone, or it will destroy you!

37 RUSH!

COMFORT ZONERS: They rush the process and do not trust the process.

OWNERS: They trust the process and do not rush the process. They understand that greatness takes time to form.

Truthfully! really truthfully, Which One Are You? Because the only person who can seriously answer this question truthfully, is YOU.

☐ Comfort Zoner
☐ Owner

Tip: Never rush greatness, it's possible. Let's Connect @KeithSmithOwner

38 LEADS!

COMFORT ZONERS: Think positive talking and thinking only leads to growth and change in their life.

OWNERS: Know that talk without action leads to no change or growth.

Truthfully! really truthfully, Which One Are You? Because the only person who can seriously answer this question truthfully, is YOU.

☐ Comfort Zoner
☐ Owner

> **Tip:** Talking and planning something without taking action on it leads to death. Let's Connect @KeithSmithOwner

MULTIPLE!

COMFORT ZONERS: Are the people that get multiple ideas and never use any of them.

OWNERS: Are the people that will get one idea, use that idea and turn it into multiple ideas.

Truthfully! really truthfully, Which One Are You? Because the only person who can seriously answer this question truthfully, is YOU.

☐ Comfort Zoner
☐ Owner

> **Tip:** Stop looking for new idea and focus on growing and expanding the idea you already have. It's possible. Let's Connect @KeithSmithOwner

OBSTACLES!

COMFORT ZONERS: Let the thoughts and obstacles in their mind stop them from growing or doing wonderful things in life.

Destroy your Comfort Zone, or it will destroy you!

OWNERS: Let the thoughts and obstacles in their mind push them to grow, expand and do more things in life.

Truthfully! really truthfully, Which One Are You? Because the only person who can seriously answer this question truthfully, is YOU.

☐ Comfort Zoner
☐ Owner

Tip: Use and look at your obstacles as being a part of helping you to build and create your vision, instead of stopping you from your vision. it's possible. Let's Connect @KeithSmithOwner

 **W**EAR!

COMFORT ZONERS: Love to wear low self-esteem and say that it brings their beauty out more. Such as makeup, fake beards, Beijing, weave, eyelashes, hair, fake butt, fake breast, fake nose, fake lips and etc. with the exception of an illness or skin defect.

OWNERS: Wear their natural look. They understand that they were created to be natural and that makeup only makes up a lie.

Truthfully! really truthfully, Which One Are You? Because the only person who can seriously answer this question truthfully, is YOU.

☐ Comfort Zoner
☐ Owner

Tip: Become confident about yourself in your natural skin, it's possible. Let's Connect @KeithSmithOwner

 # CHANGE!

COMFORT ZONERS: Fear Change.

OWNERS: Love, accept, expect and create change. They do not change to become bitter, they change to become better.

Truthfully! really truthfully, Which One Are You? Because the only person who can seriously answer this question truthfully, is YOU.

☐ Comfort Zoner
☐ Owner

Tip: You have the Power to change, Use your power. It's possible. Let's Connect @KeithSmithOwner

☆43 SHORT STORY:

YOU CANNOT

DECEIVE ME!

There was a young woman sitting at a nice restaurant. A man wearing decent clothes came in and noticed her sitting by herself.

He asked her, "Do you mind if I sit with you?"

She said, "Sure! no problem, have a seat." When he sat down, she asked him, "What's your name and what type of work do you do?"

He said "My name is John and I am in the process of looking for something to do." He then asked her, "What type of work do you do?"

She replied, "I am the owner of a large corporation. I have over 3,000 stores around the world, and I've been in business 15 years."

He said, "Wow I know that must be a lot of work and people to watch over."

She said, "Yes it is but I have my own parking spot, I can work from my home if I choose, and I make over 2 million dollars a year."

"Wow, that is amazing. I am actually looking for a job and it looks like I am talking to the right person." He replied.

"Yes, you are", she said.

With curiosity she asked, "What type of work are you looking to do?"

With excitement he replied, "Whatever you need me to do."

"Tell me a little more about yourself," she replied.

"Sure! I am an ex-crackhead, I have been married five times and am on my sixth marriage, but I'm about to get a divorce. I have seven children, but only two of them live with me. I am forty-three years old, and I have had over twenty jobs in my lifetime. My two children and soon to be ex-wife have nowhere to sleep at night."

After he finished giving her his background, she looked at him and said, "John, I apologize but I do not hire people like you in my corporation. I do not want your personality to affect any of my staff. Therefore, I have to pass on giving you a job."

John put his head down and cried.

She began to rub his back and said, "I apologize John but I just cannot bring your negative background into my establishment."

When she finished talking, John lifted up his head and said, "I am ok."

Then John looked at her and said, "I am not crying because I am hurt or because I do not have a job. I am crying because the person I hired 15 years ago, who is now a district manager of over 30 of my stores just told me that she cannot give me a job because of my past."

"I just gave you the same background story you gave my staff 15 years ago. My staff brought your story to me to see if I would hire

Destroy your Comfort Zone, or it will destroy you!

someone like you in my company and that day I said, "yes let's give her a chance."

"Tina Johnson you have lied and tried to deceive me from the moment I sat down with you."

She interrupts John and says, "Wait! How do you know my name? How did I lie and try to deceive you?"

He said, "Because I am the owner of the corporation you work for. The same corporation you said you own."

"I apologize Tina but on Monday morning, your Vice Presidents, Kaleah and Promise Smith, will help you pack your belongings."

"I no longer need a selfish, uncompassionate liar working for my corporation. Thank you and have a nice dinner. If you do not mind, I will pay for your last meal on my corporation expense, the corporation you pretended to own."

"By the way Tina, I own this restaurant that you are sitting in as well. I also own the bank that you pay your 6,000 dollar monthly mortgage to every first of the month on your 5 million dollar home. It will eventually be my home again since I no longer need you working for me. Thank you and enjoy your dinner at my expense."

Truthfully, Do you think John should have fired Tina?
□ Yes
□ No

COMFORT ZONERS: Lie about the position they are in or the company they own.

OWNERS: Do not have to lie about what they own they are humble.

PART 1: MENTALLY

Truthfully! really truthfully, Which One Are You? Because the only person who can seriously answer this question truthfully, is YOU.

☐ Comfort Zoner
☐ Owner

Tip: Stop lying about what you have and start creating what you would like to have. It's possible. Let's Connect @KeithSmithOwner

My Reflection Notes

Write down the topic number(s) that you TRUTHFULLY know
that you need to improve in and why?

PART 2

SPIRITUALLY

COMFORT ZONER overall meaning: A person who wants to change for the better BUT does not want to be a part of his/her change to become better.

OWNER overall meaning: A person who takes ownership and owns up to their responsibilities in order to create the necessary change in their life.

MY DAILY CONFESSION

I Keith Smith choose to glance at my PAST, be grateful and enjoy every moment of my PRESENT and be excited. Focus on and smile at my FUTURE, simply because I Keith Smith have the number one thing in my body that woke me up to see this day. Which is the breath that I am breathing. "Thank you Lord for the breath of LIFE."

By Keith Smith

44 THANK GOD!

COMFORT ZONERS: Thank God for another day yet they do not do anything in that day but stay in the same place as the day before.

OWNERS: Thank God for another day and they multiply, replenish and subdue the earth in that day. They have made progress from the day before.

Truthfully! really truthfully, Which One Are You? Because the only person who can seriously answer this question truthfully, is YOU.

☐ Comfort Zoner
☐ Owner

Tip: Make progress daily, it's possible. Let's Connect @KeithSmithOwner

45 CLEANLINESS!

COMFORT ZONERS: Always say, "cleanliness is next to Godliness", but their vehicles is not cleaned out, their credit is not cleaned up, there life is not cleaned up, their house is not cleaned up, their children are not cleaned up, their marriage is not cleaned up, but yet they love using the scripture "cleanliness is next to Godliness".

Destroy your Comfort Zone, or it will destroy you!

OWNERS: They say, "cleanliness is next to Godliness", so they create an atmosphere of cleanliness in their lives, they create a clean family, a clean vehicle, a clean marriage, clean house, clean credit score, a clean relationship, clean love for people and a forgiving heart towards people. They understand the power of your choice to be clean, not just to simply say "cleanliness is next to Godliness" but they create, demonstrate and operate in cleanliness.

Truthfully! really truthfully, Which One Are You? Because the only person who can seriously answer this question truthfully, is YOU.

☐ Comfort Zoner
☐ Owner

Tip: Create a Clean Atmosphere, it's possible! Let's Connect @KeithSmithOwner

 **T**OLD!

COMFORT ZONERS: Say things like, "God told me not to own things or not to work". Then go around expecting people to give them handouts such as money, cars, clothes, place to live etc.

OWNERS: Understand the power of creating what God told them to do and the power of working like God told them to. They understand that the bible says, "man does not work, man does not eat" and "God gives them power to get wealth". They clearly understand the bible never said do not work and expect handouts.

Truthfully! really truthfully, Which One Are You? Because the only person who can seriously answer this question truthfully, is YOU.

☐ Comfort Zoner
☐ Owner

> **Tip:** Get up and go to work, it's possible. Let's Connect @KeithSmithOwner

47 PROGRESS!

COMFORT ZONERS: Make excuses and no progress, they do not understand that what they do today affects their tomorrow. Their excuses of today will be their captivity for tomorrow, their excuses of today will be their stress for tomorrow, their excuses of today will lead them to become negative towards people and things of tomorrow, their excuses of today will lead them to become bitter for tomorrow, their excuses of today will have them in bondage for tomorrow, their excuses for today will not allow them to forgive someone of tomorrow and their excuses of today will have them blaming someone for their downfalls, failures and mistakes of tomorrow.

OWNERS: Make constant progress and have no excuses, they understand that what they do today affects their tomorrow. Their progress of today will be their confidence for tomorrow, their progress of today will be their prosperity for tomorrow, their progress of today will be their growth of tomorrow, their progress of today will be their happiness and joy of tomorrow, their progress of today will be their smiles of tomorrow. Their progress of faith today will be their healing for tomorrow.

Destroy your Comfort Zone, or it will destroy you!

Truthfully! really truthfully, Which One Are You? Because the only person who can seriously answer this question truthfully, is YOU.

☐ Comfort Zoner
☐ Owner

Tip: Stop making excuses and make progress, it's possible.
Let's Connect @KeithSmithOwner

 48 **P**RAY!

COMFORT ZONERS: Are the people that pray all day, every day and do not believe and trust God. Instead they decide to worry about what they prayed for if it does not happen quickly.

OWNERS: Are the people that pray and believe they will receive what they prayed for and they eventually have it. Their faith gives them their proof of results.

Truthfully! really truthfully, Which One Are You? Because the only person who can seriously answer this question truthfully, is YOU.

☐ Comfort Zoner
☐ Owner

Tip: Believe God for what you prayed for, it's possible.
Let's Connect @KeithSmithOwner

FORGIVE
AND
APOLOGIZE!

COMFORT ZONERS: When they get into an argument or have problems with their wife, husband, children or parents they do not want to forgive and apologize. They just walk out on their entire family. They are weak and cannot work out problems. The first thing they want to do when they face a problem or obstacle is give up, quit or walk out on what belongs to them.

OWNERS: When they get into arguments or have problems with their wife, husband, children or parents they quickly apologize, forgive, love and find a way to work out their problems. They are problem solvers. They understand the power of solving problems and overcoming obstacles. They also understand the power of unity and growth is formed through hardships and obstacles.

Truthfully! really truthfully, Which One Are You? Because the only person who can seriously answer this question truthfully, is YOU.

☐ Comfort Zoner
☐ Owner

Tip: Forgive quickly, it's possible. Let's Connect @KeithSmithOwner

Destroy your Comfort Zone, or it will destroy you!

50 DESIRE!

COMFORT ZONERS: Want God to give them the desire of their heart but they do not do anything to honor their God.

OWNERS: Delight themselves in the Lord and acknowledge that God gives them the desires of their heart.

Truthfully! really truthfully, Which One Are You? Because the only person who can seriously answer this question truthfully, is YOU.

☐ Comfort Zoner
☐ Owner

Tip: Delight yourself in the Lord, it's possible. Let's Connect @KeithSmithOwner

51 GOD IS

FAITHFUL!

COMFORT ZONERS: Always say things like, "God is faithful, God is in the blessing business, God is blessing me right now", but they never demonstrate or show God's faithfulness. Instead they show and demonstrate lack, doubt, fear, bondage, stress, negativity, poverty, worry, anxiety, unforgiveness, jealousy, envy, hatred, lies, pleasing themselves, fraud and scamming people for self-gain. They never show and demonstrate God's faithfulness. They just like to say how faithful God is.

OWNERS: They say things like, "God is faithful." They show and demonstrate God's faithfulness, through their ability to create because they understand God created them to create. They show and demonstrate God faithfulness through faith, love, giving, sowing and reaping, forgiving themselves and others, being patient in the process, casting their care on the Lord, vision expansion, peace of mind and in not being weary in well doing. So when they say God is faithful, they are showing and demonstrating the faithfulness of God, they understand the power in God and in faith.

Truthfully! really truthfully, Which One Are You? Because the only person who can seriously answer this question truthfully, is YOU.

☐ Comfort Zoner
☐ Owner

Tip: Demonstrate God faithfulness in your life, it's possible. Let's Connect @KeithSmithOwner

52 DOCTOR!

COMFORT ZONERS: Are the people that will go to the doctor, find out what is wrong with their body. The doctor prescribes medicine or explains a necessary procedure. They say they are not going to take that medicine or go through with the procedure because they are going to trust God for their healing.

Destroy your Comfort Zone, or it will destroy you!

Why did you go get checked out then if you are going to trust God anyway? That is why a lot of people die because they go off what people will say about them. They are programed to avoid doctors, it is like a family tradition.

OWNERS: Are the people that go to the doctor and find out what is wrong with their body and then say, "God will heal me with or without the medicine but I choose to take the medicine the doctor gave me and the word of God medicine. All while continuously trusting God for healing, they ask God to take the side effects out of the medicine even before they take it. They understand that God has healed them already. I just have to believe it and walk in it and go through the manifestation process. They trust God through it all." They use the Wisdom of God.

Truthfully! really truthfully, Which One Are You? Because the only person who can seriously answer this question truthfully, is YOU.

☐ Comfort Zoner
☐ Owner

Tip: Use the Wisdom of God, it's possible. Let's Connect @KeithSmithOwner

 **53 K**ILL!

COMFORT ZONERS: Love blaming God when something bad happens to them or someone they know. They say things like, "I am mad at God because he killed my family, friend etc." Or they say, "why would God do this bad thing to me if he loves me." Or

"why would God allow this bad situation to happen to me?" They say things like, "I am giving up on God."

OWNERS: They do not blame God for hatred and evil things that happen in their life. They blame the devil because they understand that the devil comes to kill, steal and to destroy their life but God comes to give them life more abundantly. When comfort zoners say to owners that they are giving up on God the owner ask them, "where are you going to go after you give up on love, peace, joy, healing, happiness and life which is God himself?"

Truthfully! really truthfully, Which One Are You? Because the only person who can seriously answer this question truthfully, is YOU.

- ☐ Comfort Zoner
- ☐ Owner

Tip: Never leave the presence of God, it's possible. Let's Connect @KeithSmithOwner

54 WHAT GOD

WANTS!

COMFORT ZONERS: Always tell people what God wants them to have, maintain, do and keep. Although they never actually have these things because they are to scared to receive and create what they believe God wants for their life.

Destroy your Comfort Zone, or it will destroy you!

OWNERS: They read, acknowledge and create what God wants them to create, have and be. They go where God wants them to go, they do not simply talk about what God wants them to create, have and maintain, they create it.

Truthfully! really truthfully, Which One Are You? Because the only person who can seriously answer this question truthfully, is YOU.

☐ Comfort Zoner
☐ Owner

Tip: Stop waiting and start creating, it's possible. Let's Connect @KeithSmithOwner

55 HEAL!

COMFORT ZONERS: Say, "Lord heal the people, so they can stop hurting me".

OWNERS: Say, "Lord heal me, so I can stop allowing the people to hurt me. Whether it is physically, emotionally, financially, mentally, spiritually or naturally. I need to be healed."

Truthfully! really truthfully, Which One Are You? Because the only person who can seriously answer this question truthfully, is YOU.

☐ Comfort Zoner
☐ Owner

Tip: Allow God to Heal YOU, it's possible. Let's Connect

PROMOTE!

COMFORT ZONERS: Seek after people and things for them to promote them in their life.

OWNERS: Seek God for Him to promote them in their life.

Truthfully! really truthfully, Which One Are You? Because the only person who can seriously answer this question truthfully, is YOU.

☐ Comfort Zoner
☐ Owner

Tip: Stop giving people power over you to control your destiny, it's possible. Let's Connect @KeithSmithOwner

MAKE **I**T!

COMFORT ZONERS: Go to and depend on owners to know how to make it in life.

OWNERS: Go to and depend on God and their creative thinking to know how to make it in life.

Truthfully! really truthfully, Which One Are You? Because the only person who can seriously answer this question truthfully, is YOU.

Destroy your Comfort Zone, or it will destroy you!

□ Comfort Zoner
□ Owner

Tip: Depend on God, it's possible. Let's Connect @KeithSmithOwner

 # 58 DEVIL!

COMFORT ZONERS: Always blame the devil for their failures. They say things such as, "the devil just tempted me and made me do this or that." That is the devils job, to tempt you and to steal, kill and destroy your character and soul, but it is your choice to give in to it or not.

OWNERS: They do not blame the devil, they resist the devil because they understand for every temptation that the devil brings to them, God gives them a way to escape. That is why they are able to create and conquer because they submit unto God and resist the devil.

Truthfully! really truthfully, Which One Are You? Because the only person who can seriously answer this question truthfully, is YOU.

□ Comfort Zoner
□ Owner

Tip: Resist the devil through prayer, it's possible. Let's Connect @KeithSmithOwner

ACCORDING!

COMFORT ZONERS: Operate According to Time and Fear.

OWNERS: Operate According to Grace and Faith.

Truthfully! really truthfully, Which One Are You? Because the only person who can seriously answer this question truthfully, is YOU.

☐ Comfort Zoner
☐ Owner

Tip: Operate in faith, it's possible. Let's Connect @KeithSmithOwner

DOUBT!

COMFORT ZONERS: Walk in doubt and disbelief.

OWNERS: Walk in faith and belief. They get rid of doubt, so they can continue to create and expand.

Truthfully! really truthfully, Which One Are You? Because the only person who can seriously answer this question truthfully, is YOU.

☐ Comfort Zoner
☐ Owner

Destroy your Comfort Zone, or it will destroy you!

BIBLE!

COMFORT ZONERS: Read the bible so that they can argue and debate with other people about what the bible says.

OWNERS: Read the bible so that they can get an understanding and obey the word of God.

Truthfully! really truthfully, Which One Are You? Because the only person who can seriously answer this question truthfully, is YOU.

☐ Comfort Zoner
☐ Owner

CHOOSE!

COMFORT ZONERS: Think they choose God.

OWNERS: Know God chose them and they receive God in their heart.

Truthfully! really truthfully, Which One Are You? Because the

only person who can seriously answer this question truthfully, is YOU.

☐ Comfort Zoner
☐ Owner

Tip: God chose you, it's possible. Let's Connect @KeithSmithOwner

63 MAILBOX!

COMFORT ZONERS: Wait on and hope to get a prophecy about a check coming in their mailbox.

OWNERS: Go out and create checks to come into their mailbox.

Truthfully! really truthfully, Which One Are You? Because the only person who can seriously answer this question truthfully, is YOU.

☐ Comfort Zoner
☐ Owner

Tip: Go out and create, operative word is GO. It's possible. Let's Connect @KeithSmithOwner

64 KNOWLEDGE!

COMFORT ZONERS: Listen to and accept knowledge from people who do not have any knowledge of God.

Destroy your Comfort Zone, or it will destroy you!

OWNERS: Listen to and accept knowledge and advice from people who have knowledge of God. Owners understand the power of influence through listening to something or someone and reading. Owners understand what you continuously listen to and read is who and what you aspire to become.

Truthfully! really truthfully, Which One Are You? Because the only person who can seriously answer this question truthfully, is YOU.

□ Comfort Zoner
□ Owner

Tip: Be mindful of who you accept knowledge from, it's possible.
Let's Connect @KeithSmithOwner

 **E**XPECT!

COMFORT ZONERS: Expect change and things from God but they do not want to change for God.

OWNERS: Understand that in order to change, they have to be involved and a part of their change. They have to do something and not just sit and expect change to happen or to come to them.

Truthfully! really truthfully, Which One Are You? Because the only person who can seriously answer this question truthfully, is YOU.

□ Comfort Zoner
□ Owner

Tip: You create your change, it's possible. Let's Connect @KeithSmithOwner

 66 PRAY FOR!

COMFORT ZONERS: Like to pray for themselves to get an understanding and know who they are.

OWNERS: Like to pray for themselves to get an understanding and know who God is. They say, "if I know who God is he will show me who I am supposed to be and what I am supposed to be doing."

Truthfully! really truthfully, Which One Are You? Because the only person who can seriously answer this question truthfully, is YOU.

□ Comfort Zoner
□ Owner

Tip: Get to know God through prayer and the word of God, it's possible. Let's Connect @KeithSmithOwner

67 ENCOURAGE!

COMFORT ZONERS: Get encouraged by someone reading the bible. They say things such as, continue to read your bible because that is really helping people understand who God is.

OWNERS: Get encouraged when people demonstrate what is in the bible. They say things such as, continue reading and demonstrating what is in the bible, because that is really helping people see and understand who God really is.

Truthfully! really truthfully, Which One Are You? Because the only person who can seriously answer this question truthfully, is YOU.

☐ Comfort Zoner
☐ Owner

Tip: Demonstrate the bible, it's possible. Let's Connect @KeithSmithOwner

68 LEADERSHIP!

COMFORT ZONERS: Think leadership is about being served and not serving.

OWNERS: Understand that leadership is learning how to follow and serve others.

Truthfully! really truthfully, Which One Are You? Because the only person who can seriously answer this question truthfully, is YOU.

☐ Comfort Zoner
☐ Owner

Tip: Follow great leaders, it's possible. Let's Connect @KeithSmithOwner

 **THEM!**

COMFORT ZONERS: Sit and wait on God to bring things to them.

OWNERS: Go out and get what God has already created for them.

Truthfully! really truthfully, Which One Are You? Because the only person who can seriously answer this question truthfully, is YOU.

☐ Comfort Zoner
☐ Owner

Tip: Stop waiting and go out and get. Operative word is GO, it's possible. Let's Connect @KeithSmithOwner

Destroy your Comfort Zone, or it will destroy you!

 PEOPLE!

COMFORT ZONERS: Are the people that want many things but get very little. They do not do anything, that is why they get nothing.

OWNERS: Are the people that get a lot because they work diligently with their hands and also with their mind to create.

Truthfully! really truthfully, Which One Are You? Because the only person who can seriously answer this question truthfully, is YOU.

☐ Comfort Zoner
☐ Owner

Tip: Do something productive, it's possible. Let's Connect @KeithSmithOwner

SHORT STORY

"I WANT TO BE JUST LIKE HIM!"

I want to be just like him. I want to be just like him, with the cars he drives, the house he lives in, I want to be just like him. I love when I see him and how he takes care of his wife. He buys her the finest clothes and the nicest cars. His kids go to the best schools. I want to be just like him. Every time I see him, as he walks into his 13 bedroom house, with the picket fence and the nice cars. Ferrari, Lamborghini, Bugatti and Maserati is what he rides around in. I want to be just like him. That man doesn't even go to work. He owns his own company. The people that approach him are always shaking his hand and saying to themselves "Wow! I just want to be a part of him." I want to be just like him. I even want my kids to be just like his kids. So the person I want to be like, he finally approaches me.

He asks, "How are you doing young man?" I responded, "I'm alright, but what about you?"

He said, "I'm perfectly fine but trust me young man I want to be like you."

I sighed deeply and said, "Hold on! Not me! I want to be just like you."

He corrected me and said, "Young man, I'm not talking about being just like you. I want to have what you have, but not do what you do." I said "Sir, personally, I want to be just like you. I see the way you treat your wife, how you buy her the finest clothes and live in the nicest house. I want to be just like you. I see the way you take care and dress your kids with the nicest clothes and put them in a house with a picket fence. I want to be just like you."

He interrupts me quickly. "Young man listen to me. The things you see they are only a facade that you can only see, but please don't try to compete. He said "Young man, listen to me! That wife that you see of mine, with the nice cars and the nice clothes! She trying to find the door that she can leave out of, because every night I'm beating her. You may ask why I beat her? Because every night she tries to leave me. She says I have the nicest house but don't spend time with her. So what do I do? She says "I have all the luxury things that your money can buy me but I don't have you." I understand my kids go to the best schools but I don't have time for them. The business I built and own requires too much time and I don't have time for them.

Destroy your Comfort Zone, or it will destroy you!

"They wear the nicest clothes and go to the best schools, however, you are looking at the outer appearance of me. You don't know what's behind all this. You are looking at what I have, what I drive and what my wife dresses like. You don't understand the thoughts that are inside of me. Every night I feel strife. Every night I go to the bathroom and think about taking my own life. The bitter that's inside of me, you wouldn't understand if it's wrong or right. You are saying you want to be just like me? Young man, trust me, you really don't. I need love and peace in my heart, is that what you really want? I need to love people and not be envy towards the people that try to slander my name. You want to be just like me but the things you're seeing with your eyes are false fame."

"You see me with the nicest cars and the nicest clothes, you say you want to be just like me but you do not know exactly what I do behind closed doors. You do not know what is inside of me young man, every night I think about taking my own life. What is inside of me is filled with a lot of strife. Do not let outside appearances define who you want to be like. Honestly you should want to be like the one that is above, Jesus Christ. The man above does not have any flaws, but instead you are trying to be just like a man that is on earth with many flaws. You need to focus on trying to be just like the bigger power who is God. Young man listen to me, never say you want to be just like a man on earth, from this point on start striving to be just like the man that created the whole universe. Look up to the sky and say I want to be just like Him, you God the one that created the whole universe, the man who gives love unconditionally. The man that gives so much joy. The man that will help you when you are really hurting. The man that will help you when you are really broken. He will bring your family back together. Listen to me. You saying you want to be just like me but I encourage you to be just like God. Strive to be like the one that saved your life, the one that loves you, that died for you, and cares for you who is Jesus Christ. There is nothing wrong with saying

PART 2: SPIRITUALLY
78

that you like a person's character and you would not mind implementing some of their character, into yourself, but from this point on never say you want to be just like somebody. God has made you unique in your own body, so know that you are somebody and do not let anybody tell you different. Understand the person that you are. You are somebody so do not try to be just like him. He might want to be just like you, but from this point on continue to follow and be just like Christ and no one else. Do this or you will be fooled."

My Reflection Notes

Write down the topic number(s) that you TRUTHFULLY know
that you need to improve in and why?

PART 3

PHYSICALLY

COMFORT ZONER overall meaning: A person who wants to change for the better BUT does not want to be a part of his/her change to become better.

OWNER overall meaning: A person who takes ownership and owns up to their responsibilities in order to create the necessary change in their life.

DO AS YOU DO

Stop getting mad at people who copy exactly what you do. Just because they may copy exactly what you do or have the same skills as you, does not mean that they have the same brain, vision, character, personality, anointing, and ambition as you do to build what you have built or what you are building.

By Keith Smith

I FIRED MY BOSS!

COMFORT ZONERS: Say things like, "I fired my boss. Now I can work for myself from home." The only difference is that their boss is not in the company building with them anymore. Instead their boss has just arrived in their comfort zone place now, their home. They did not fire their boss, they simply changed bosses by changing locations and position. If you are not the founder or creator of the company, you are labeled as a comfort zoner not an owner. No matter how you or anyone else tries to make you believe that you are your own boss. Ask yourself, "do I have the power to shut this company down if I choose?" If your answer is no, you are not the owner you are the comfort zoner. Stop deceiving yourself and stop letting other people deceive you, by having you think that you own or are part owner of the company, that you are really working for. You are not building your dreams, you are really being deceived and helping your boss build his/her dreams.

OWNERS: Say things like "I fired my boss. Now I created my own company so comfort zoners can work from home and drive people, deliver medicine and different products in their own vehicles for me. File their own taxes, so I don't have to keep up with all of their paper trail." If you are the founder and creator of your company you are labeled as an owner not a comfort zoner.

Truthfully! really truthfully, Which One Are You? Because the only person who can seriously answer this question truthfully, is YOU.

Destroy your Comfort Zone, or it will destroy you!

□ Comfort Zoner
□ Owner

73 KEY!

COMFORT ZONERS: Are happy to have the key to unlock the company door. So that they can go in and lock the company door behind themselves before closing up.

OWNERS: Are the people that created the key and the company door that the comfort zoners can go in and out of, to lock and unlock it behind themselves. They say things like, "I'm happy that the comfort zoners are happy to have my company key that I created for them. I am happy that I make more physical hard labor and work for them to open up and close my company and none for me. They say things like, I can enjoy my life and my freedom now, since I have comfort zoners opening and locking the doors to my company that I created for them to maintain."

Truthfully! really truthfully, Which One Are You? Because the only person who can seriously answer this question truthfully, is YOU.

□ Comfort Zoner
□ Owner

STATES!

COMFORT ZONERS: When you tell them that they have to work in a different state, they say things like, "Wow! That is too far for me. I have to stay close to where I live."

OWNERS: When owners say that they have work in different states, they say "That is not too far for me because I hire comfort zoners to go and work for me."

Truthfully! really truthfully, Which One Are You? Because the only person who can seriously answer this question truthfully, is YOU.

☐ Comfort Zoner
☐ Owner

Tip: Become omnipresent by owning the company and not just working for a company, it's possible. Let's Connect @KeithSmithOwner

15 YEARS!

COMFORT ZONERS: Say things like, "this company needs me. I have been here over 15 years and nobody can take over my position and job, no one can do my job better than I can. If they get rid of me they are not going to know what to do."

OWNERS: As an owner you say things like, "I will replace you and train someone else to do the work you have been doing and they will do an even better job than you have for over 15 years. You are easily replaceable."

Truthfully! really truthfully, Which One Are You? Because the only person who can seriously answer this question truthfully, is YOU.

☐ Comfort Zoner
☐ Owner

Tip: Create something! So you can become the replacer instead of replaceable, it's possible. Let's Connect @KeithSmithOwner

 # 76 PICTURE!

COMFORT ZONERS: Take a picture of the company they work for.

OWNERS: Take a picture of the company they own.

Truthfully! really truthfully, Which One Are You? Because the only person who can seriously answer this question truthfully, is YOU.

☐ Comfort Zoner
☐ Owner

Tip: Create your own to take pictures of. It's possible! Let's Connect @KeithSmithOwner

 # CLOCK!

COMFORT ZONERS: Have to rush in and punch somebody else's clock for work.

OWNERS: Create the clock that comfort zoners have to punch in for work.

Truthfully! really truthfully, Which One Are You? Because the only person who can seriously answer this question truthfully, is YOU.

☐ Comfort Zoner
☐ Owner

Tip: Create the time, it's possible. Let's Connect
@KeithSmithOwner

 # DEDICATED!

COMFORT ZONERS: Believe life is limited. Their life is dedicated to working and punching the owner's clock to help the owner succeed and have freedom.

OWNERS: Believe life is unlimited. Their life is dedicated to using their brain to build and create their company. They then hire comfort zoners to use their physical body and do their physical work while they enjoy everyday life.

Truthfully! really truthfully, Which One Are You? Because the

Destroy your Comfort Zone, or it will destroy you!

only person who can seriously answer this question truthfully, is YOU.

□ Comfort Zoner
□ Owner

Tip: Begin to enjoy everyday life, it's possible. Let's Connect @KeithSmithOwner

VISION!

COMFORT ZONERS: Work for people who followed their dreams and vision.

OWNERS: Work on and follow their own dreams and vision.

Truthfully! really truthfully, Which One Are You? Because the only person who can seriously answer this question truthfully, is YOU.

□ Comfort Zoner
□ Owner

Tip: Create your own vision so others can maintain it for you, it's possible. Let's Connect @KeithSmithOwner

PART 3: PHYSICALLY

STEP OUT!

COMFORT ZONERS: Wait to see what someone else is going to say or do first. Then that is when they step out and jump on the bandwagon and say things like, "I was going to say that, I was thinking about that or I was going to do that." They are procrastinators and blessing missers.

OWNERS: Step out and make moves happen, period.

Truthfully! really truthfully, Which One Are You? Because the only person who can seriously answer this question truthfully, is YOU.

☐ Comfort Zoner
☐ Owner

> **Tip:** Create things to happen, don't just wait on things to happen. It's possible! Let's Connect @KeithSmithOwner

RETIRE!

COMFORT ZONERS: Say, "go work for a nice paying company with great benefits that you can retire from, after twenty five to forty years of your hard physical labor you put in." Now you have to wait on your check every month instead of weekly or bi-weekly, that is sad.

OWNERS: Say, "I'm building a company with nice pay and great

Destroy your Comfort Zone, or it will destroy you!

benefits that comfort zoners can retire from, after twenty five to forty years of their physical and hard labor to build for me I am getting paid every minute without ever touching work."

Truthfully! really truthfully, Which One Are You? Because the only person who can seriously answer this question truthfully, is YOU.

☐ Comfort Zoner
☐ Owner

Tip: Create a company with benefits, it's possible.
Let's Connect @KeithSmithOwner

WHEN TIMES GET HARD!

COMFORT ZONERS: Always want to be like an owner and have what owners have, but they do not want to grind, sweat, get criticized by critics, make mistakes, experience plenty of failures throughout life process, experience losing clients, people and things, experience not making money in the beginning stages of the process, experience paying out more than receiving, experience giving away their service for free or discounts sometimes in order to gain more business down the line and experience going through the process for preparation like an owner. So when times get hard, they go back and get a job instead of creating a job in hard times. You will never be an owner with that mindset.

OWNERS: When times get hard, they do not go get a job. They create jobs in hard times so that those hard times for them turn into great times for them.

Truthfully! really truthfully, Which One Are You? Because the only person who can seriously answer this question truthfully, is YOU.

☐ Comfort Zoner
☐ Owner

Tip: Don't give up because of pressure, instead create while under pressure. It's possible! Let's Connect @KeithSmithOwner

83 CONNECTED!

COMFORT ZONERS: Always say who someone else should get connected to and never connect themselves. They say things such as, "this person should get connected to this person and they will eventually make it in whatever they are trying to do."

OWNERS: Find a way to get connected to who they need to be connected to, so they can create the environment they want or dreamed of. Owners understand that they are the connection and blueprint to the puzzle while everyone else are the pieces to make the puzzle whole.

Truthfully! really truthfully, Which One Are You? Because the only person who can seriously answer this question truthfully, is YOU.

Destroy your Comfort Zone, or it will destroy you!

☐ Comfort Zoner
☐ Owner

Tip: Find a way to get connected to who you need to be connected to. So your vision can expand and grow, it's possible.
Let's Connect @KeithSmithOwner

84 CHORES LIST!

COMFORT ZONERS: Do not make a cleaning list for their home. They just clean whenever they feel like it.

OWNERS: Create a list of chores to follow in order Monday thru Sunday for their home, because they understand the more they maintain their home, the less cleaning and stress they have to go through by keeping it clean. Owner's also understand that they can think better when their homes are clean.

Truthfully! really truthfully, Which One Are You? Because the only person who can seriously answer this question truthfully, is YOU.

☐ Comfort Zoner
☐ Owner

Tip: Create a chore cleaning list, it's possible and very important
Let's Connect @KeithSmithOwner!

Example of an owner's cleaning chore list sheet:

Monday thru Sunday

1. Kitchen: dishes, stove, counters, table, microwave.

2. Living Room: clean tables, mirrors.

3. Family Bathroom: tub, toilet, mirrors, sink.

4. Bedroom: Straighten top of dresser, clean mirrors, make up bed.

5. Sweep: Kitchen, living room, family room, bedroom.

6. Vacuum: living room, bedroom.

7. Once a Week: mop floors, clean out refrigerator.

8. Once a Month: clean and organize closets, organize inside of dressers and organize cabinets.

My Cleaning Chore List
Use this list as an example to create your own cleaning chore list. It's Possible!

Morning Cleaning Chores Duties

Schedule for the week of_____ to _____.

Duties clean	Monday	Tuesday	Wednesday	Thursday	Friday	Saturday	Sunday
Tub							
Sink							
Mirror							
Washer & Dryer							
Livingroom Table							
Stove							
Microwave							
Refrigerator							
Dishes							
Fix Couch							
Sweep Floor							
Change Garbage							
Fix Bed							
Room Sink							
Room Mirror							
Room Toilet							
Sweep room floor							
Empty room trash							
Fix Promise bed							
Mop floor O.A.W.							
Send Quote							
Read Bible Chapter							

"With God All Things Are Possible" Matthew 19:26

"No matter how hard it is or how hard it get, I'M GOING TO MAKE IT! I EXPECT GREAT THINGS TO HAPPEN TO ME TODAY! IT'S POSSIBLE!"

ACCOMPLISH!

COMFORT ZONERS: Go through life day by day trying to accomplish things. They say things like, "I can never get around to doing this or that, it is too much for me to do."

OWNERS: Go through life accomplishing things little by little. They understand the power of making a to do list and checking off what they have completed daily. They never use the term "I can never get around to do this or that", because what they have to do is on their to do list and being checked off. A disorganized person will soon come to poverty.

Truthfully! really truthfully, Which One Are You? Because the only person who can seriously answer this question truthfully, is YOU.

☐ Comfort Zoner
☐ Owner

Tip: Create a to-do-list to accomplish daily, it's possible.
Let's Connect @KeithSmithOwner

ROUTINE!

COMFORT ZONERS: Just wake up at whatever time they feel like it and guess what they are going to do after they wake up, they do not set a routine to how their morning is going to go.

OWNERS: They create a routine to how their morning is going to go before they get their entire day started. They understand that routines are important to do because it helps them to prepare for that day.

Truthfully! really truthfully, Which One Are You? Because the only person who can seriously answer this question truthfully, is YOU.

☐ Comfort Zoner
☐ Owner

Tip: Create a daily routine, it's possible. Let's Connect @KeithSmithOwner

Example #1 of a True Routine:
I "Keith Smith" Arise at 3:00A.M Every Morning

Study My Bible
Exercise> 30 Minutes
Take Shower
Put On My Clothes
Eat Breakfast
Read A Positive Book

Clean House/Attend to
Morning Chore List
Work On Goal Project
Write Out My "To Do List" For Today
Get My Day Started

Example #2 of a True Routine:
I "Kaleah Smith" Arise at 5:00A.M Every Morning

Take Shower
Clean Tub
Put My Clothes, Earrings and Perfume on.
Get School Lunch Ready.
Do My Hair
Eat Breakfast
Brush My Teeth

Make Up My Bed
Check Backpack for Homework.
Repeat Scripture Matthew 7:7 and Goals 3 Times "No Matter What."
Write Out My "To Do List" For Today
Get My Day Started

My Morning Daily Routine List

Use this example to create your own list

Time	Mon	Tues	Wed	Thurs	Fri
3:00am	Study Bible	Study Bible	Study Bible	Study Bible	Study Bible
3:30am	Exercise> 30 Minutes	Exercise> 30 Minutes	Exercise> 30 Minutes	Exercise> 30 Minutes	Exercise> 30 Minutes
4:05am	Get Dressed	Get Dressed	Get Dressed	Get Dressed	Get Dressed
4:45am	Eat Breakfast	Eat Breakfast	Eat Breakfast	Eat Breakfast	Eat Breakfast
5:00am	Read A Positive Book	Read A Positive Book	Read A Positive Book	Read A Positive Book	Read A Positive Book
5:30am	Clean House	Clean House	Clean House	Clean House	Clean House
6:30am	Work on Goal Project	Work on Goal Project	Work on Goal Project	Work on Goal Project	Work on Goal Project
7:30am	Do "To Do List" For Today	Do "To Do List" For Today	Do "To Do List" For Today	Do "To Do List" For Today	Do "To Do List" For Today
8:00am	Get My Day Started	Get My Day Started	Get My Day Started	Get My Day Started	Get My Day Started
9:00pm	BEDTIME	BEDTIME	BEDTIME	BEDTIME	BEDTIME

Destroy your Comfort Zone, or it will destroy you!

OWN!

COMFORT ZONERS: Does not own anything.

OWNERS: Own comfort zoners families, house, vehicle, credit score, attitude, peace of mind, their time, their thinking, their mindset, their money, their financial freedom, their personal freedom, their vacations and their lifestyle. They own these things simply because they own the number one thing in their lives, which is the clock they punch in for work to make their living.

Truthfully! really truthfully, Which One Are You? Because the only person who can seriously answer this question truthfully, is YOU.

☐ Comfort Zoner
☐ Owner

Tip: You were born to create and own things. Start taking control of your own life today, it's possible. Let's Connect @KeithSmithOwner

GOAL!

COMFORT ZONERS: Goal is to work hard for a company now so they can retire and try to find time to do what they want to for themselves later.

OWNERS: Goal is to work hard and build their company now, so they can enjoy their family later. While comfort zoners maintain and retire from their company they are focused on building now.

Truthfully! really truthfully, Which One Are You? Because the only person who can seriously answer this question truthfully, is YOU.

☐ Comfort Zoner
☐ Owner

> **Tip:** Put your time, years and energy into building and creating something that you can pass down to your children's children. It's possible. Let's Connect @KeithSmithOwner

PAID!

COMFORT ZONERS: Work the hardest and the most and get paid less.

OWNERS: Work less or do not work at all and get paid more.

Truthfully! really truthfully, Which One Are You? Because the only person who can seriously answer this question truthfully, is YOU.

☐ Comfort Zoner
☐ Owner

> **Tip:** Create your own net worth. Instead of letting someone else determine what you are worth, it's possible. Let's Connect @KeithSmithOwner

FAKE SMILE!

COMFORT ZONERS: Fake smiles when the owner shows up or is around, just to try to be liked or get a promotion.

OWNERS: Do not need to fake a smile. They just show up to their establishments, complement their comfort zone workers on their great work and performance. Then they implement what needs to be changed and accomplished in their company.

Truthfully! really truthfully, Which One Are You? Because the only person who can seriously answer this question truthfully, is YOU.

☐ Comfort Zoner
☐ Owner

Tip: Get rid of the fake smiles. Because fake smiles don't promote you. Creating and owning something for yourself is what can and will promote you, it's possible. Let's Connect @KeithSmithOwner

ENVIRONMENT!

COMFORT ZONERS: Complain about their environment and surrounding.

OWNERS: Talk, create, and change their environment and surroundings.

Truthfully! really truthfully, Which One Are You? Because the only person who can seriously answer this question truthfully, is YOU.

☐ Comfort Zoner
☐ Owner

Tip: Stop complaining and decide to create a Change now, it's possible. Let's Connect @KeithSmithOwner

# PROOF!

COMFORT ZONERS: Have no proof of what they are doing. They just talk about what they are doing or going to do. They are loud mouths but their lifestyle is on stop and mute.

OWNERS: Have proof of what they are doing. Just look at their lifestyle and what they have. They move in silence but their lifestyle and actions are the proof that speaks loudly.

Truthfully! really truthfully, Which One Are You? Because the only person who can seriously answer this question truthfully, is YOU.

☐ Comfort Zoner
☐ Owner

Tip: Let your mouth speak less and your actions speak more, it's possible. Let's Connect @KeithSmithOwner

Destroy your Comfort Zone, or it will destroy you!

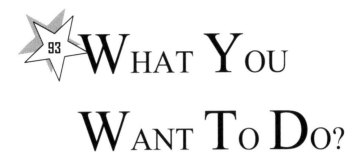

WHAT YOU WANT TO DO?

COMFORT ZONERS: Go through life trying to figure out what they want to do.

OWNERS: Go through life knowing what they want to do. They want to keep creating, building and owning up to their responsibilities and companies so that comfort zoners can continue working for them while they enjoy everyday life.

Truthfully! really truthfully, Which One Are You? Because the only person who can seriously answer this question truthfully, is YOU.

☐ Comfort Zoner
☐ Owner

Tip: Stop going through life like you are an accident waiting to happen. Instead go through life creating what you would like to see happen for you and in you. It's possible. Let's Connect @KeithSmithOwner

94 BELIEVE!

COMFORT ZONERS: Want people to believe in them before they get started on something.

OWNERS: Get started on things and then watch comfort zoners believe in them.

Truthfully! really truthfully, Which One Are You? Because the only person who can seriously answer this question truthfully, is YOU.

☐ Comfort Zoner
☐ Owner

Tip: Just get started. Everything and everyone else will eventually follow you after you get started, it's possible. Let's Connect @KeithSmithOwner

95 BUSY!

COMFORT ZONERS: Are busy watching television and feeding their mind and eyes with foolishness and empty entertainment, such as reality shows, sports, bad news etc.

OWNERS: Are busy creating the reality shows, sports etc. that comfort zoners are watching. Owners do not have time to feed their mind with that foolishness or empty entertainment. They just invest in creating it to make a profit. An owner's mindset is the more comfort zoners keep feeding their mind and watching this foolishness and empty entertainment, the more they will keep creating and getting paid from it. They will continue telling their vision (television) through comfort zoners minds and eyes.

Truthfully! really truthfully, Which One Are You? Because the only person who can seriously answer this question truthfully, is YOU.

☐ Comfort Zoner
☐ Owner

Tip: Be careful of what you read and listen to, it's possible. Let's Connect @KeithSmithOwner

 # PERFECT!

COMFORT ZONERS: Wait on the perfect moment.

OWNERS: Create their perfect moment.

Truthfully! really truthfully, Which One Are You? Because the only person who can seriously answer this question truthfully, is YOU.

☐ Comfort Zoner
☐ Owner

Tip: Create your perfect moments, it's possible. Let's Connect @KeithSmithOwner

97 DREAM!

COMFORT ZONERS: Say to owners in the beginning of their creation, that what you are creating is a pipe (crackhead) dream.

OWNERS: Make what was a pipe (crackhead) dream to comfort zoners, become the right dream for them. They then hire the comfort zoners pipe (crackhead) dreamers to work for them, the right dreamers.

Truthfully! really truthfully, Which One Are You? Because the only person who can seriously answer this question truthfully, is YOU.

☐ Comfort Zoner
☐ Owner

Tip: Make your pipe (crackhead) dream to others. Become your right dream to you, it's possible. Let's Connect @KeithSmithOwner

98 OLD SELF!

COMFORT ZONERS: Say "go back to being your old self."

OWNERS: Say, "my old self is what had me in the comfort zoners place."

Truthfully! really truthfully, Which One Are You? Because the only person who can seriously answer this question truthfully, is YOU.

Destroy your Comfort Zone, or it will destroy you!

☐ Comfort Zoner
☐ Owner

Tip: Continue evolving into greatness and leave your old self in the past, it's possible. Let's Connect
@KeithSmithOwner

 # No Call

No Show!

COMFORT ZONERS: They have to go to work. If they decide to go out to eat with no call or no show to their company, they will be fired.

OWNERS: They are the type of people that can go out with comfort zoners and have something to eat with them, while still getting paid and do not have to call or show for work.

Truthfully! really truthfully, Which One Are You? Because the only person who can seriously answer this question truthfully, is YOU.

☐ Comfort Zoner
☐ Owner

Tip: Create your freedom, it's possible. Let's Connect
@KeithSmithOwner

PART 3: PHYSICALLY

MAINTAIN!

COMFORT ZONERS: Are janitors. They maintain the work that the owners created.

OWNERS: Are creators. They create the work for the comfort zoners to maintain.

Truthfully! really truthfully, Which One Are You? Because the only person who can seriously answer this question truthfully, is YOU.

☐ Comfort Zoner
☐ Owner

Tip: Become a creator, it's possible. Let's Connect @KeithSmithOwner

STRUGGLES!

COMFORT ZONERS: Look at struggles and obstacles as a stop sign for them to stop.

OWNERS: Look at struggles and obstacles as an opportunity for them to grow, expand, and to continue moving forward and upward.

Truthfully! really truthfully, Which One Are You? Because the only person who can seriously answer this question truthfully, is YOU.

Destroy your Comfort Zone, or it will destroy you!

□ Comfort Zoner
□ Owner

 # HOUSE!

COMFORT ZONERS: Have to find time to do things. Find time to go to their children events, go to the hospital if their kids are sick, clean their house up, fix their credit and etc.

OWNERS: Set time to do things. Set time to go on trips, clean their house, go to their children games and etc. owners have plenty of time. They hire the comfort zoners that have to find time, to work for them with their physical labor while they set time to enjoy their everyday lives and their families lives.

Truthfully! really truthfully, Which One Are You? Because the only person who can seriously answer this question truthfully, is YOU.

□ Comfort Zoner
□ Owner

MOTIVATE!

COMFORT ZONERS: Wait to feel motivated or be motivated to get started on something or even to continue doing something.

OWNERS: Do not wait for something or someone to motivate them to get started. They become their own self-motivation to start and to continue moving forward until they complete their goal.

Truthfully! really truthfully, Which One Are You? Because the only person who can seriously answer this question truthfully, is YOU.

☐ Comfort Zoner
☐ Owner

Tip: Can't nobody stop you but YOU, It's Possible. Let's Connect @KeithSmithOwner

CALL!

COMFORT ZONERS: Call the company they work for and check in for work.

OWNERS: Call the company they own and check on their work.

Truthfully! really truthfully, Which One Are You? Because the only person who can seriously answer this question truthfully, is YOU.

☐ Comfort Zoner
☐ Owner

Tip: Create something to check on, it's possible. Let's Connect
@KeithSmithOwner

105 EXCUSE!

COMFORT ZONERS: Find an excuse to avoid work.

OWNERS: They find a way to create work.

Truthfully! really truthfully, Which One Are You? Because the only person who can seriously answer this question truthfully, is YOU.

☐ Comfort Zoner
☐ Owner

Tip: Find a way to accomplish things, it's possible. Let's Connect
@KeithSmithOwner

106 WAKE UP!

COMFORT ZONERS: Have to wake up to go to work.

OWNERS: Choose to wake up to check on the comfort zoners at work.

Truthfully! really truthfully, Which One Are You? Because the only person who can seriously answer this question truthfully, is YOU.

☐ Comfort Zoner
☐ Owner

> **Tip:** Create a choice of freedom, it's possible. Let's Connect @KeithSmithOwner

# **L**IGHT!

COMFORT ZONERS: Are the people that go in a dark room and wonder where the light is.

OWNERS: Are the people that go in a dark room and create the light.

Truthfully! really truthfully, Which One Are You? Because the only person who can seriously answer this question truthfully, is YOU.

☐ Comfort Zoner
☐ Owner

> **Tip:** Stop complaining and start creating because you are the light, so turn it on. It's Possible. Let's Connect @KeithSmithOwner

Destroy your Comfort Zone, or it will destroy you!

COMMITTED!

COMFORT ZONERS: Show themselves to be committed, but not proven. They show up every day but spend their time gossiping, being jealous of other people, and are lazy. Expect to be promoted because they are committed to showing up at work, church, event, seminar, etc.

OWNERS: Show themselves to be committed and proven. They show up every day and do the work, bring peace, improve, expand and grow.

Truthfully! really truthfully, Which One Are You? Because the only person who can seriously answer this question truthfully, is YOU.

☐ Comfort Zoner
☐ Owner

Tip: Do the work and not just show up for the work, it's possible. Let's Connect @KeithSmithOwner

PROMOTION!

COMFORT ZONERS: Are promotion receivers.

OWNERS: Are promotion givers.

Truthfully! really truthfully, Which One Are You? Because the only person who can seriously answer this question truthfully, is YOU.

☐ Comfort Zoner
☐ Owner

Tip: Become a promotion giver, it's possible. Let's Connect @KeithSmithOwner

 **H**ARD!

COMFORT ZONERS: Work hard.

OWNERS: Play hard from comfort zoners hard work.

Truthfully! really truthfully, Which One Are You? Because the only person who can seriously answer this question truthfully, is YOU.

☐ Comfort Zoner
☐ Owner

Tip: Create a lifestyle to be able to play hard, it's possible. Let's Connect @KeithSmithOwner

Destroy your Comfort Zone, or it will destroy you!

PARENT

TEACHER

CONFERENCE!

COMFORT ZONERS: Do not like to go to their child's parent teacher conference because as a parent they are ashamed how they will be dressed or look and if their children will be embarrassed with their parents appearance. They feel that they do not have a great education or vocabulary to talk to their child's teacher. They do not want to hear how bad their child is doing in class, they do not want to take off work or they simply, do not care about their child's education. It is sad when a parent is not interested in what was birthed from them or what they adopted. They would rather email or call the teacher to have a parent teacher conference over the phone as though they can visibly see how their child's class looks, a place their child is attending on a daily basis.

OWNERS: Understand that it is a must to be present at parent teacher conference. It is important that they schedule that day off no matter how they are dressed or how they look as the parent, no matter if their child is going to be embarrassed with their appearance, no matter how bad or good their child is doing in school or what education and vocabulary they have as a parent. One thing owners understand is that, their children can have straight "A's and one "B" but as the parent they still have to see their child's teacher face to face, see what their child's classroom looks like, see where their child sits at in the classroom, see and hear what their child's strengths and weaknesses are in each class and see what their child needs improvement in. So that they can help their children work on and continue to improve. They understand that their child can have "A's and one "B" on their report card but he/she can be a class clown, showing up late for class, ditching class, sleeping in class and etc. That is why owners love to go to parent teacher conference because they can find out from the teachers how their child is really doing in their class separate from what their child tells them when they get home from school every day.

Truthfully! really truthfully, Which One Are You? Because the only person who can seriously answer this question truthfully, is YOU.

□ Comfort Zoner
□ Owner

Tip: Get rid of all of your excuses and attend your children parent teacher conference, it's possible. Let's Connect @KeithSmithOwner

BUSY -VS -

PRODUCTIVE!

There is a big difference between being busy and being productive. A lot of people confuse these two with each other and think that they are synonyms, when in actuality they are antonyms.

Destroy your Comfort Zone, or it will destroy you!

Being Busy= Confusion, stress, no direction, depression, stable, no growth, multitasking etc.

Being Productive= Growth, expansion, strategy, direction, multi-focusing, focusing on the WIN (What's Important Now) before taking on another task. Not trying to do everything, but focusing on the right thing.

People think doing a lot of activities and being physically involved in a lot of things is being productive. Being busy is a distraction when you're not accomplishing anything.

COMFORT ZONERS: Are busy.

OWNERS: Are productive.

Truthfully! really truthfully, Which One Are You? Because the only person who can seriously answer this question truthfully, is YOU.

☐ Comfort Zoner
☐ Owner

Tip: Stay Productive. It's Possible! Let's Connect @KeithSmithOwner

 **T**RIED!

COMFORT ZONERS: Say they are trying to do something.

OWNERS: They do not try, they make it happen.

Truthfully! really truthfully, Which One Are You? Because the

only person who can seriously answer this question truthfully, is YOU.

☐ Comfort Zoner
☐ Owner

Tip: Stop trying and just do it, it's possible. Let's Connect @KeithSmithOwner

 # RESPECT!

COMFORT ZONERS: Disrespect people but want everybody to respect them.

OWNERS: Understand in order to get respect they have to first give respect. They understand the power of sowing and reaping.

Truthfully! really truthfully, Which One Are You? Because the only person who can seriously answer this question truthfully, is YOU.

☐ Comfort Zoner
☐ Owner

Tip: Give respect to be respected, it's simple and possible. Let's Connect @KeithSmithOwner

STARTED!

COMFORT ZONERS: Are the people that need everything to get started when they have an idea.

OWNERS: Are the people that just need an idea to get started. They understand that they have the main two things to get started, themselves and their brain. They start where they are, use what they have and create to get more of what they need in the process of what they are doing.

Truthfully! really truthfully, Which One Are You? Because the only person who can seriously answer this question truthfully, is YOU.

☐ Comfort Zoner
☐ Owner

Tip: Just get started with what you have now. Everything else will come as long as you stay committed and focused, It's possible.
Let's Connect @KeithSmithOwner

FOOLISHNESS!

COMFORT ZONERS: Entertain and pay attention to negativity, foolishness and garbage.

OWNERS: They ignore foolishness, negativity and garbage. Owners understand you defeat foolish people with intelligence. Just ignore the foolishness and the foolish people.

Truthfully! really truthfully, Which One Are You? Because the only person who can seriously answer this question truthfully, is YOU.

☐ Comfort Zoner
☐ Owner

Tip: Ignore the foolishness, it's possible. Let's Connect @KeithSmithOwner

# BUILD!

COMFORT ZONERS: Are like construction workers. They use their physical body and labor to help build the building and maintain the building.

OWNERS: Are like architects. They use their brain to draw out and create the building for the comfort zoners to build and maintain. Architects live longer because they do not use their physical body to do the labor, they use their brain to create the labor that needs to be done by the Comfort Zoners.

Truthfully! really truthfully, Which One Are You? Because the only person who can seriously answer this question truthfully, is YOU.

☐ Comfort Zoner
☐ Owner

Tip: Exercise your brain by using it to create things, it's possible. Let's Connect @KeithSmithOwner

Destroy your Comfort Zone, or it will destroy you!

GIVEN!

COMFORT ZONERS: Wait on work to be given to them.

OWNERS: Go out and create work for themselves.

Truthfully! really truthfully, Which One Are You? Because the only person who can seriously answer this question truthfully, is YOU.

☐ Comfort Zoner
☐ Owner

Tip: Stop waiting for what you want to happen in your life and start creating what you want to happen in your life. It's possible! Let's Connect @KeithSmithOwner

SHOW UP!

COMFORT ZONERS: Show up late to an event or service and want a front row seat or the best service.

OWNERS: Show up early and follow the rules that are given to them. That is why they receive everything given to them.

Truthfully! really truthfully, Which One Are You? Because the only person who can seriously answer this question truthfully, is YOU.

☐ Comfort Zoner
☐ Owner

SOMETHING!

COMFORT ZONERS: Work jobs that they do not want. They thank God for something they are scared to change or leave. They say I am going to be grateful for something they are giving their service grudgingly to.

OWNERS: Do not create jobs they do not like. If they do not like what they created, they simply create something new. No complaining.

Truthfully! really truthfully, Which One Are You? Because the only person who can seriously answer this question truthfully, is YOU.

☐ Comfort Zoner
☐ Owner

EVENTS!

COMFORT ZONERS: Show up to events to be seen.

OWNERS: Show up to events to be involved and make a difference.

Destroy your Comfort Zone, or it will destroy you!

Truthfully! really truthfully, Which One Are You? Because the only person who can seriously answer this question truthfully, is YOU.

☐ Comfort Zoner
☐ Owner

Tip: Make a difference, it's possible. Let's Connect @KeithSmithOwner

SUNDAYS!

COMFORT ZONERS: Have to work on Sundays if their owner tells them to. They have no choice if they want to keep working for that owner.

OWNERS: Can go to church on Sundays if they choose to because they have the Comfort Zoners working for them.

Truthfully! really truthfully, Which One Are You? Because the only person who can seriously answer this question truthfully, is YOU.

☐ Comfort Zoner
☐ Owner

Tip: Become your own boss so you can have the privilege of scheduling the days you will have off, it's possible. Let's Connect @KeithSmithOwner

123 TRIP!

COMFORT ZONERS: In order for them to take a trip, they have to get permission from their owner. They ask the owner questions like, "how long is my vacation pay?"

OWNERS: Take trips when they choose. They have no job that needs to be informed. No one to get permission from. They have the comfort zoners working for them while they take trips and enjoy everyday life.

Truthfully! really truthfully, Which One Are You? Because the only person who can seriously answer this question truthfully, is YOU.

☐ Comfort Zoner
☐ Owner

Tip: Create an everyday enjoyable life, it's possible. Let's Connect @KeithSmithOwner

124 DEGREE!

COMFORT ZONERS: Go to college to receive a degree or certificate, in order to work for some owners company.

OWNERS: Create the degree and certificate to give to the comfort zoners after the completion of their course. Owners do not have to go to college if they choose not to. They just continue hiring and paying the college graduates. Nothing against anyone who chose to go to college.

Truthfully! really truthfully, Which One Are You? Because the only person who can seriously answer this question truthfully, is YOU.

☐ Comfort Zoner
☐ Owner

Tip: Earn a Degree to create and own something of your own, it's possible. Let's Connect @KeithSmithOwner

 **B**EST!

COMFORT ZONERS: Love to say, "my best is yet to come."

OWNERS: Say, "my best comes at the moment I choose to change, start planning and working towards it."

Truthfully! really truthfully, Which One Are You? Because the only person who can seriously answer this question truthfully, is YOU.

☐ Comfort Zoner
☐ Owner

Tip: Your Best is not coming if you are waiting on it. Your best will come when you start to create it. So create it, it's possible. Let's Connect @KeithSmithOwner

INTO!

COMFORT ZONERS: Put their energy into their past.

OWNERS: Put their energy into their future, because they understand what you keep watering will eventually grow and what you stop watering will eventually die. That is why owners do not put energy/water into their past.

Truthfully! really truthfully, Which One Are You? Because the only person who can seriously answer this question truthfully, is YOU.

☐ Comfort Zoner
☐ Owner

Tip: Let your past be your past. Now focus on creating and building your future, it's possible. Let's Connect @KeithSmithOwner

TIME!

COMFORT ZONERS: Do not respect time.

OWNERS: Value, respect and cherish time, because owners understand one can never get back the time that has been wasted.

Truthfully! really truthfully, Which One Are You? Because the only person who can seriously answer this question truthfully, is YOU.

Destroy your Comfort Zone, or it will destroy you!

☐ Comfort Zoner
☐ Owner

Tip: Control your time. do not let time control you, it's possible. Let's Connect @KeithSmithOwner

 # 128 **P**LEASE!

COMFORT ZONERS: Are under everyone and have to please everyone at the owner's company. They have to please the vice president, district manager, general manager, assistant manager, manager, supervisor, hiring manager and many more. They say things like, "here comes my boss, let me act like I'm really working and give a fake smile."

OWNERS: Are over everyone at their company. They do not have to please anyone. They just show up at their company when they choose to.

Truthfully! really truthfully, Which One Are You? Because the only person who can seriously answer this question truthfully, is YOU.

☐ Comfort Zoner
☐ Owner

Tip: Stop giving everyone power over you. Create something of your own, it's possible. Let's Connect @KeithSmithOwner

129 BED!

COMFORT ZONERS: Have to go to bed early and wake up at a certain time because they have to go punch the owner's clock.

OWNERS: Can choose to decide what time they would like to go to bed and wake up, because they do not have to punch the clock. They can choose to go jogging, walking or even for breakfast in the morning. They know they have comfort zoners waking up in the morning to take care of the work for them.

Truthfully! really truthfully, Which One Are You? Because the only person who can seriously answer this question truthfully, is YOU.

☐ Comfort Zoner
☐ Owner

Tip: Create choices, it's possible. Let's Connect @KeithSmithOwner

130 SLAVES

MASTERS!

COMFORT ZONERS: Are slaves. No matter how you look at it you are still a slave. You have to ask your boss if you can leave, can you take the day off, can you go to your children's event, can you go to your hospital appointment, you get paid less than what you are really worth, no work, no pay and etc.

OWNERS: Are masters, they are the ones that pay the comfort zoners for their hard physical labor. They are the ones that let the comfort zoners leave, take the day off from work, go to their children event, hospital appointments etc. when they choose to let them.

Truthfully! really truthfully, Which One Are You? Because the only person who can seriously answer this question truthfully, is YOU.

☐ Comfort Zoner
☐ Owner

Tip: Break free from that slave bondage mentality and create something to master over, it's possible. Let's Connect @KeithSmithOwner

131 GARBAGE!

COMFORT ZONERS: Maintain and clean up the owners garbage.

OWNERS: Create the garbage and pay the Comfort Zoners to clean their garbage up.

Truthfully! really truthfully, Which One Are You? Because the only person who can seriously answer this question truthfully, is YOU.

☐ Comfort Zoner
☐ Owner

LAID OFF!

COMFORT ZONERS: Work long years and lots of hours at the owner's company and still have to be concerned if they may be getting laid off, replaced, fired or suspended. Even though they work very hard throughout the year and they make the owners millions of dollars, they still have to go to work wondering if that is going to be the day that they get fired when they punch in.

OWNERS: Never have to worry if they are going to get laid off or fired because they own the company.

Truthfully! really truthfully, Which One Are You? Because the only person who can seriously answer this question truthfully, is YOU.

☐ Comfort Zoner
☐ Owner

Destroy your Comfort Zone, or it will destroy you!

WATCH!

COMFORT ZONERS: Like to watch owner's create things.

OWNERS: Like to watch comfort zoners work in or for their creation.

Truthfully! really truthfully, Which One Are You? Because the only person who can seriously answer this question truthfully, is YOU.

☐ Comfort Zoner
☐ Owner

> **Tip:** Create something to be watched over, it's possible.
> Let's Connect @KeithSmithOwner

PROCESS!

COMFORT ZONERS: Like to rush the process.

OWNERS: Like to have patience for the process they are creating.

Truthfully! really truthfully, Which One Are You? Because the only person who can seriously answer this question truthfully, is YOU.

☐ Comfort Zoner
☐ Owner

135 NOTHING!

COMFORT ZONERS: When they are working at someone else's company or even in their own personal lives they say things like, "if there's nothing for me to do, that's exactly what I'm going to do; nothing." That is why they never get promoted or receive a pay raise because of their do nothing mentality.

OWNERS: Say, "if there is nothing for me to do, then I am going to find and create something, not only for me to enjoy but for comfort zoners to enjoy and have something to do as well."

Truthfully! really truthfully, Which One Are You? Because the only person who can seriously answer this question truthfully, is YOU.

☐ Comfort Zoner
☐ Owner

136 APPLY!

COMFORT ZONERS: Read books just to say that they read. But do not apply what they have read to their everyday life. They just like to look smart, intelligent, sound good and have great conversation but do not seek real change.

OWNERS: Read books to apply what they have read to their everyday life. So they can grow and expand in their life and vision. Owners do not simply look for great conversations, they look for great creations and ideas through conversations.

Truthfully! really truthfully, Which One Are You? Because the only person who can seriously answer this question truthfully, is YOU.

☐ Comfort Zoner
☐ Owner

Tip: Read to apply! not to just read, it's possible. Let's Connect @KeithSmithOwner

137 PROJECT!

COMFORT ZONERS: Like to hear people say, "wow that is going to be good," when they tell someone about their idea or project that they are working on. When someone asks them how long they have been planning to start on their project, they say about ten years. They just like to be heard and think that they are doing the work and accomplishing goals just by talking about the project and getting compliments.

OWNERS: They like to work in silence and make things a reality. When they ask the comfort zoners, "how long have you been working on this project?", and a comfort zoners say ten years-owners tend to walk away because they understand the power of procrastination, they also understand that spending time speaking to a procrastinator can lead to the same effect on their personality.

So they do not encourage a procrastinators idea, they just walk away from it so it won't taint their thinking or their creativity.

Truthfully! really truthfully, Which One Are You? Because the only person who can seriously answer this question truthfully, is YOU.

☐ Comfort Zoner
☐ Owner

Tip: Talk less and focus more, it's possible. Let's Connect @KeithSmithOwner

 # LIKE!

TRUE STORY

COMFORT ZONERS: Like to shout to be heard and not change anything. They speak loudly but their actions are on mute.

OWNERS: Like to be quiet and create things in silence. Their actions speak loud but their mouth is on mute.

Truthfully! really truthfully, Which One Are You? Because the only person who can seriously answer this question truthfully, is YOU.

☐ Comfort Zoner
☐ Owner

TRUE STORY: My sister Levita (Vita) who is a year older than my twin Kyle Smith (Author of "Questions We All Have Regarding Relationships" Available on Amazon.com) taught me

Destroy your Comfort Zone, or it will destroy you!

that I can do ANYTHING with no excuses. I saw her walk across the stage to receive her Registered Nurse (RN) college degree at DePaul University, while working a full time job as a CNA (Certified Nurse Assistance), with six children and also had to take care of her wifely duties as well. She INSPIRED me to be DETERMINED no matter what obstacles come my way. I always speak highly about Vita to people everywhere I go because I have never met anyone with that much ambition and enthusiasm. When I was in the audience looking at my sister Vita walking across that stage I shed a tear because I knew her story. This wasn't just ANYBODY walking across that stage. This was somebody with six children who still didn't let obstacles stop her.

Trust me when I say there were many obstacles trying to stop her, I really mean it. There were many things trying to get in her way. Every. Single. Day. But that didn't stop her. She kept pushing forward, and with tears in her eyes, she finally completed what she had set out to accomplish. Even though she felt abated plenty of days and wanted to stop and give up she kept moving forward and upward. The thing about my sister Vita that is so AMAZING to me is that when she's working on something her mouth is on MUTE, but her actions and results speak LOUDLY.

Keep it up sister. You have proven and shown me that there's no one who can stop you in this world but you. I love you big sister. You demand people to move out of your way or step to the side when you are coming through because you are so driven. Your ambition and determination cannot be matched.. I love you Vita.

Tip: Be quiet and just work. Everybody doesn't need to know what you are doing. Go owner up, it's possible. Let's Connect @KeithSmithOwner

PART 3: PHYSICALLY

My Reflection Notes

Write down the topic number(s) that you TRUTHFULLY know
that you need to improve in and why?

My Reflection Notes

Write down the topic number(s) that you TRUTHFULLY know
that you need to improve in and why?

PART 4

FINANCIALLY

COMFORT ZONER overall meaning: A person who wants to change for the better BUT does not want to be a part of his/her change to become better.

OWNER overall meaning: A person who takes ownership and owns up to their responsibilities in order to create the necessary change in their life.

FINANCES

Make everyday a productive day and count it all joy, because what you deposit into your future today, you can withdraw from it tomorrow. "NO deposit, NO withdraw".

By Keith Smith

139 TWO GUYS!

There were two guys, one named Patrick and the other named Mike. Patrick owns 15 hotels and Mike is a retired electrician collecting a check of $11,000 every month. Every day Mike and Patrick went to the park faithfully for 4 years straight. They also went on extravagant vacations once a month. They would sit at the park, feed the ducks, barbecue and talk. The more they went to sit at the park and on extravagant vacations, over time one became homeless without letting his friend know and the other one became very wealthy.

Which One Became Homeless?
☐ Patrick
☐ Mike

Tip: Stop trying to do extravagant things on a set and no more growth income, it's possible. Let's Connect @KeithSmithOwner

140 SHOULDERS!

COMFORT ZONERS: Walk with their shoulders high and their head lifted up. All the while they are broke, owing people money, in debt, living paycheck to paycheck, taking orders from the owner of the company and have the nerve to look down on other people.

OWNERS: Walk with their shoulders high and their head lifted up. Their credit is good, they live financially free day to day and have comfort zoners working for them. The only time they look down on someone is when they are lifting them up.

Truthfully! really truthfully, Which One Are You? Because the only person who can seriously answer this question truthfully, is YOU.

☐ Comfort Zoner
☐ Owner

Tip: Put your shoulders down and create yourself a way out of bondage, it's possible. Let's Connect @KeithSmithOwner

MONEY, MONEY, MONEY!

COMFORT ZONERS: Say, "you do not need money to be happy. Money does not make you happy."

OWNERS: Say, "get some money and you will see for yourself. Poverty does not make you happy either."

Truthfully! really truthfully, Which One Are You? Because the only person who can seriously answer this question truthfully, is YOU.

□ Comfort Zoner
□ Owner

Tip: If money doesn't make you happy, give yours away to somebody that it will make happy. If you have some, It's possible Let's Connect @KeithSmithOwner.

142 SAY!

COMFORT ZONERS: Always say what other people should and should not do, have and not have with their money. "They should give it to the poor, give it to charity or build shelters with their money." They say things such as, "they do not need that big house. Why do they need that many cars? They can give some of those cars to somebody else that is in need of a car, they know they are living above their means, trying to keep up with the Jones and they can be helping the homeless by giving them food instead of throwing food away."

Comfort zoners always get an idea for other people's wealth. They say what Oprah, Bill Gates, Tyler Perry, Steve Harvey, Floyd Mayweather Jr. and many more should be doing with their wealth.

OWNERS: Always say, "hey, it is my money, I made it, I choose to do what I want to with my money. I choose to give my money or what I have to whoever I want to. I choose to get the cars or how many cars I like because I made the money for it. I choose to stay in the neighborhood that I like because I made the money to afford to stay where I like to.

Comfort zoners mind your own business and create your own wealth so you can start choosing who and where you want to give your money to. Comfort zoners you can own something too. Own

Destroy your Comfort Zone, or it will destroy you!

minding your "own" business and not everyone else's. Comfort zoners why don't you create something to give to the people you keep saying other people should be giving to. Owners understand the process of people creating what they made belongs to them and whoever they choose to share it with.

Truthfully! really truthfully, Which One Are You? Because the only person who can seriously answer this question truthfully, is YOU.

☐ Comfort Zoner
☐ Owner

Tip: Make it your business to mind your own business, it's possible. Let's Connect @KeithSmithOwner

143 INCOME TAX

MONEY!

COMFORT ZONERS: When they get their income tax money, they get more in debt because they have to impress people that really do not care about them or what they have anyway. So they spend their income tax money on clothes for themselves and one to two outfits for their children, if they have any children. They go and put a down payment on a car, that will eventually get repossessed six months later after their purchase date, because the job they work is not enough to cover the monthly payments, insurance, gas and maintenance on the vehicle they purchased. Then they become broke until their next pay period.

OWNERS: When they get their income tax money, they try to get out of debt if they have any and get their credit score higher. So they pay off some debt and bills that they owe, they buy their children clothes, put money to the side to save, take their children on a trip, find something to invest their income tax money into so they make more money or even put their whole income tax towards their rent for the year. Owners understand income tax money only comes once a year in a mass amount, so they do not waste their tax money but they make their tax money work for a great benefit to help their children and themselves.

Truthfully! really truthfully, Which One Are You? Because the only person who can seriously answer this question truthfully, is YOU.

☐ Comfort Zoner
☐ Owner

Tip: Use your income tax money to create something that will generate more money for yourself. Now your money is making money for you, it's possible. Let's Connect @KeithSmithOwner

144 CHARGE!

COMFORT ZONERS: Say things like, "hey I am not going to charge you for that service I did for you because I do not want to miss out on my blessing."

OWNERS: Say things like, "comfort zoners already missed out on their blessing when they do not charge or receive from a person. They do not understand the power of giving and receiving. That is why they are broke now and working for people because they do not know how to accept what is being given to them for their work, talent or gift that they have performed or given out." Owners understand that God is the one that blesses them whether they accept a payment from someone or not for the service they perform.

Truthfully! really truthfully, Which One Are You? Because the only person who can seriously answer this question truthfully, is YOU.

☐ Comfort Zoner
☐ Owner

Tip: Stop being afraid to charge and accept payments from people for your service given, it's possible. Let's Connect @KeithSmithOwner

145 ENOUGH!

COMFORT ZONERS: Feel and say they never make enough.

OWNERS: When they feel that they are not making enough they start creating enough and more such as, companies, food, homes, money and more.

Truthfully! really truthfully, Which One Are You? Because the only person who can seriously answer this question truthfully, is YOU.

☐ Comfort Zoner
☐ Owner

Tip: Stop blaming people and create for yourself what you think enough is for you, it's possible. Let's Connect

ALLERGIC!

COMFORT ZONERS: Are scared of and allergic to success.

OWNERS: Are scared of and allergic to poverty.

Truthfully! really truthfully, Which One Are You? Because the only person who can seriously answer this question truthfully, is YOU.

☐ Comfort Zoner
☐ Owner

Tip: Look at the success as being your amazing friend and poverty as being your worst enemy, it's possible. Let's Connect @KeithSmithOwner

MONDAY!

COMFORT ZONERS: When you ask them on Mondays. "How is the day going?" they say things like, "well it's Monday. You know how Mondays can be, got to work, the weekend was too short, I can't wait for Friday," or "Friday can't get here any quicker."

OWNERS: When you ask them on Mondays, "how is the day going?" They say, "I am enjoying everyday life. I am making money on this day without touching any work, my Mondays are always great."

Truthfully! really truthfully, Which One Are You? Because the only person who can seriously answer this question truthfully, is YOU.

☐ Comfort Zoner
☐ Owner

Tip: Make everyday a productive day and count it all of joy, it's possible. Let's Connect
@KeithSmithOwner

UNEMPLOYMENT!

COMFORT ZONERS: Can get laid off any day, anytime and always have to depend on the unemployment pay.

OWNERS: Create work for the unemployment pay seeker. Owners do not value the comfort zoners opinion unless it's valuable for their company. They just hire them to stay stable at their company and take orders.

Truthfully! really truthfully, Which One Are You? Because the only person who can seriously answer this question truthfully, is YOU.

☐ Comfort Zoner
☐ Owner

Tip: Stop depending on unemployment pay to take care of you and create your own net worth, it's possible. Let's Connect
@KeithSmithOwner

149 SPENDING MONEY!

COMFORT ZONERS: Have to wait on a weekly, bi-weekly or monthly check from the owner. Have to create a budget they cannot simply spend money until they receive their next check from the owner. comfort zoners have to carefully spend their money.

OWNERS: Can freely spend money from comfort zoners hard work and labor. They can spend cheerfully because they know they are going to get back that same day what they had spent on themselves or their families. They have comfort zoners working hard for their company to replace what they had spent on them and their families.

Truthfully! really truthfully, Which One Are You? Because the only person who can seriously answer this question truthfully, is YOU.

☐ Comfort Zoner
☐ Owner

Tip: You have the power to create the times and the amount you would like to get paid. Use your power, it's possible.
Let's Connect @KeithSmithOwner

RAISE!

COMFORT ZONERS: Get $1 to $6 raise a year. They say things to their owner such as, "this is all I get for the year, for all my hard labor I put in this year."

OWNERS: Can get unlimited raises for the year, it depends on them. However much they want to make. Have you ever heard the saying "you get paid for what you work for" that saying only applies to owners not comfort zoners. Comfort zoners get what the owner gives them.

Truthfully! really truthfully, Which One Are You? Because the only person who can seriously answer this question truthfully, is YOU.

☐ Comfort Zoner
☐ Owner

Tip: Stop giving people the power to pay and promote you when they get ready to, it's possible. Let's Connect @KeithSmithOwner

BUSINESS!

COMFORT ZONERS: Get into business only to make money. They think money is more important than building relationships with people.

OWNERS: Get into business to build short term and long term relationships, because owners understand if they build great relationships, the money will come with it and possibly lifetime friends as well. Owners know that building relationships with people is more important than money.

Truthfully! really truthfully, Which One Are You? Because the only person who can seriously answer this question truthfully, is YOU.

☐ Comfort Zoner
☐ Owner

Tip: Build relationships not just one time commission, it's possible. Let's Connect @KeithSmithOwner

 **D**IE!

COMFORT ZONERS: Say, "I spend my money." They spend all of their money or put it in a savings account to be spent when they are ready. Their mindset is that "money is to be spent not stored." They say, "I cannot take it with me when I die, so I am going to enjoy and spend all of it while I am alive."

OWNERS: Say, "I grow my money, by investing and creating things, so it can become more money for my children and their children while I am living and for when I die." My money and comfort zoners that work for me, make more money for me.

Truthfully! really truthfully, Which One Are You? Because the only person who can seriously answer this question truthfully, is YOU.

Destroy your Comfort Zone, or it will destroy you!

☐ Comfort Zoner
☐ Owner

Tip: Save something for your children children's, it's possible.
Let's Connect @KeithSmithOwner

LOOK!

TRUE STORY:

COMFORT ZONERS: Look straight ahead in order to stay focused on helping themselves.

OWNERS: Look to the right and left to see who is around that they can help to become a better person and improve in their vision.

Truthfully! really truthfully, Which One Are You? Because the only person who can seriously answer this question truthfully, is YOU.

☐ Comfort Zoner
☐ Owner

TRUE STORY: My twin brother Kyle Smith Author of "Questions We All Have Regarding Relationships" (Available on Amazon.com) is one of the many people who has invested a lifetime of knowledge into my life. Kyle is the one who taught me how to iron my clothes in the middle of my 9th grade high school year. He kept a nice crease in his pants, the middle of his shirts, down both of his sleeves, the neck part of his shirts whether he was wearing a tee shirt or a collar shirt. He would iron his basketball outfit before going out to play as well. When I used to watch Kyle iron his clothes, I would try to duplicate him, but my clothes would still come out wrinkled. One day I said "Hey Kyle, can you teach me how to iron my clothes?" He said "Yeah, twin". My twin brother spent an hour of his time upstairs at our mom's house, which was called the "boys room" teaching me step by step and taking me through the process of ironing my clothes to make them look exactly like his. I mean, it was truly a process. He taught me how long to let the iron heat up before using it, exactly how much starch to spray on my clothes so they will not have a shining look to them, and so much more. Thank you twin brother for that "lifetime investment of knowledge". You did not only invest in me but you also invested in others through me, by teaching them what you took the time out to teach me. I realize that my twin spent his time teaching me something that will pass down from generation to generation. I LOVE YOU Kyle.

When Kyle taught me how to iron and crease my clothes in the middle of my 9th grade high school year, I started getting a lot of compliments from people in my classrooms on how nice my clothes were. My twin also helped me to realize through him teaching and investing in me that there is nobody on this earth that is self-made because we all had and have somebody to teach us what we know. However, a lot of people do not give full credit to those who have invested in us, because we want the credit ourselves. If you can think about everything you have learned from a newborn baby, up until your current age, someone (likely many people) taught you what you know. Whether you try to say God taught you what you know, which can be true but He uses a human being on this earth to teach us. We, as selfish people like to say God taught us, so we won't give credit to the person to whom it is due to on this earth.

I want to thank everyone who has taught me something that I

needed to know for my life journey. Every time I iron my clothes, my twin brother Kyle always pops up in my mind. Because he did not make a onetime investment in me. But he made a lifetime investment in me. So my question now becomes, who are thinking about you every time they do something because of your positive lifetime investment that you've imparted into them? The answer is not for you to figure out. It's for you to continue imparting into people's lives Lifetime Positive Investments "LPI" daily, whether it's through your positive words or demonstration of your lifestyle. Love you twin brother Kyle Smith.

Tip: Take some time out of your productive schedule to invest in someone else's life, it's possible. Let's Connect @KeithSmithOwner

My Reflection Notes

Write down the topic number(s) that you TRUTHFULLY know
that you need to improve in and why?

My Reflection Notes

Write down the topic number(s) that you TRUTHFULLY know
that you need to improve in and why?

PART 5:

EMOTIONALLY

COMFORT ZONER overall meaning: A person who wants to change for the better BUT does not want to be a part of his/her change to become better.

OWNER overall meaning: A person who takes ownership and owns up to their responsibilities in order to create the necessary change in their life.

LORD I'M

Lord I'm GRATEFUL for the things that you have blessed me with. I'm THANKFUL for the things that you haven't blessed me with and I RECEIVE the things that you are going to Bless me with. In Jesus Name Amen. Thank God.

By Keith Smith

ACKNOWLEDGE!

COMFORT ZONERS: Look for people to acknowledge and thank them for what they are doing. They say things like, "they should at least thank me for what I am doing." Stop looking for acknowledgement from people because that is what you got hired for, to do the work asked of you. Just do your job with honesty and integrity.

OWNERS: Look for people to build and work for them on what they are creating. Owners couldn't care less about people acknowledging and thanking them, as long as comfort zoners work for them, that is all that matters to them.

Truthfully! really truthfully, Which One Are You? Because the only person who can seriously answer this question truthfully, is YOU.

☐ Comfort Zoner
☐ Owner

Tip: Acknowledge and validate yourself, it's possible.
Let's Connect @KeithSmithOwner

NO!

COMFORT ZONERS: Are afraid to tell people no. They feel guilty if they say no, so instead they just accept a lot of things that they do not want or need in their life. They do a lot of things they really do not want to do. They go places they really do not want to go. They call people they really do not want to call, simply because they want to be liked by everyone and are afraid to simply say no.

OWNERS: Are not afraid to tell people no. They understand the power of growth and true friendship comes from not accepting what they do not want in their life. True friends will still be friends even if you tell them no that you cannot and will not do something for them. Owners understand the power of not trying to be accepted by people or trying to please people.

Truthfully! really truthfully, Which One Are You? Because the only person who can seriously answer this question truthfully, is YOU.

☐ Comfort Zoner
☐ Owner

Tip: There's power in the answer NO, use it. It's possible.
Let's Connect @KeithSmithOwner

 **W**ITH!

COMFORT ZONERS: Show up with the best outfits and are broke, upset, owe everyone they know, low self-esteem and are a paycheck away from losing everything.

OWNERS: Show up with the best or worst outfits and are wealthy because they have comfort zoners working for them to help them stay wealthy.

Truthfully! really truthfully, Which One Are You? Because the

only person who can seriously answer this question truthfully, is YOU.

☐ Comfort Zoner
☐ Owner

Tip: Create a wealthy mindset, it's possible. Let's Connect @KeithSmithOwner

157 **B**ASED **O**N!

COMFORT ZONERS: Make decisions based on emotions and feelings.

OWNERS: Make decisions based on principles and instincts, because owners understand making decisions off of emotions and sympathy can be a bad investment for their company or even for their life.

Truthfully! really truthfully, Which One Are You? Because the only person who can seriously answer this question truthfully, is YOU.

☐ Comfort Zoner
☐ Owner

Tip: Put your principles over your emotions, it's possible. Let's Connect @KeithSmithOwner

158 IT'S OK!

COMFORT ZONERS: Say things like, "it is okay to be down sometimes, feel bad sometimes, feel sad sometimes, go through stress sometimes, be bitter sometimes, live in fear sometimes, be unforgiving sometimes, get revenge sometimes, give up sometimes and etc." comfort zoners have a being defeated attitude.

OWNERS: Say, "it is ok to thrive all the time, overcome situations all the time, live in abundance all the time, forgive all the time, walk by faith all the time, apologize all the time, pray all the time, stay committed all the time, stay faithful and not have a giving up attitude all the time." Owners have a conquering attitude and understand the power of defeating their defeat.

Truthfully! really truthfully, Which One Are You? Because the only person who can seriously answer this question truthfully, is YOU.

☐ Comfort Zoner
☐ Owner

Tip: Defeat your defeats, it's possible. Let's Connect @KeithSmithOwner

159 SOMETHING!

COMFORT ZONERS: Say things like, "everybody does not need to own something or everybody was not created to own. Some of us were created to work for people, but at the same time they say everyone wants and needs freedom."

OWNERS: Say, "whoever would like to own something it is in them to own." They say, "until people own something they will never have freedom." They understand when they own a company they own their time, freedom and their families. They understand that people who want to own something, are the ones that go out and create their freedom.

Truthfully! really truthfully, Which One Are You? Because the only person who can seriously answer this question truthfully, is YOU.

☐ Comfort Zoner
☐ Owner

Tip: Create freedom starting now for you and your children children's, it's possible. Let's Connect @KeithSmithOwner

⭐160 Self Help!

COMFORT ZONERS: Say that they need self-help but they really do not want to be helped. They just want to talk about the help they need. They do not want to get a book and read on self-help they just really want self-pity, self-negativity, self-bondage etc. They really do not want self-help.

OWNERS: When they need self-help, they create self-help. They read books like the one you are reading right now. They seek counseling and go to seminars. They just do not say they need help but they search and get help in whatever area in their life that they need help in, whether it is spiritual, physical, mental, financial or

Destroy your Comfort Zone, or it will destroy you!

emotional help. They get help.

Truthfully! really truthfully, Which One Are You? Because the only person who can seriously answer this question truthfully, is YOU.

☐ Comfort Zoner
☐ Owner

Tip: Create self-help, it's possible. Let's Connect @KeithSmithOwner

LOOK DOWN!

COMFORT ZONERS: Look down on other people as if they are better than them. They are very negative and always look to compete against people who are not competing against them.

OWNERS: Only look down on someone is when they are picking and building them up with positive words.

They are very positive and never have to compete against anyone because they are confident about themselves.

Truthfully! really truthfully, Which One Are You? Because the only person who can seriously answer this question truthfully, is YOU.

☐ Comfort Zoner
☐ Owner

Tip: Help others to become a better them, it's possible. Let's Connect @KeithSmithOwner

 Hourly Pay!

COMFORT ZONERS: Complain about their hours and their hourly pay, as if they were the only employee that works for the company. They say I am doing more work than pay, they should pay me more.

OWNERS: Have multiple people they are paying. Owners tell comfort zoners, create your own company and you can determine what you want to get paid. If not, then simply continue to work and accept the orders and hourly payment given. Owners fire comfort zoners that are simply complaining and hire comfort zoners that will comply by their company's rules.

Truthfully! really truthfully, Which One Are You? Because the only person who can seriously answer this question truthfully, is YOU.

☐ Comfort Zoner
☐ Owner

Tip: Stop complaining and start changing, it's possible.
Let's Connect @KeithSmithOwner

163 WRITE UPS!

COMFORT ZONERS: Are three warnings or three write ups away from losing their job, home, vehicle, phones and even their family. After comfort zoners get fired from their job, they go to another company and get another job with the same three warnings and three write ups rule.

OWNERS: Do not worry about warnings or write ups. When they lose one job, they do not sweat it because they have hundreds and thousands of jobs. If they lose one job, they go get fifty more jobs that same day.

Truthfully! really truthfully, Which One Are You? Because the only person who can seriously answer this question truthfully, is YOU.

☐ Comfort Zoner
☐ Owner

Tip: Stop letting people control your destiny and future , it's possible. Let's Connect @KeithSmithOwner

I AM OUT OF HERE!

COMFORT ZONERS: Say things like, "I am done with this job, I am out of here, you are not paying me enough money" or "I can't take this anymore."

OWNERS: Have plenty of applications on file to hire someone else for when the comfort zoners quit. So they never sweat and worry about who leaves or walks out on their company.

Truthfully! really truthfully, Which One Are You? Because the only person who can seriously answer this question truthfully, is YOU.

☐ Comfort Zoner
☐ Owner

Tip: Stop complaining and start changing, it's possible.
Let's Connect @KeithSmithOwner

RESTROOM!

COMFORT ZONERS: Say, "stop thinking you are better than me. We all have to go to the restroom alike and die alike. You are not better than me."

OWNERS: Say, "I am not trying to be better than you or like you.

Destroy your Comfort Zone, or it will destroy you!

I am growing from your mistakes and actions you choose to stay in." Owners do not have to get permission to go to the restroom, do not have to rush back to work from the restroom and do not have to worry about what is taking them so long in the restroom. They do not go to the restroom unlike, comfort zoners use this restroom saying to keep them in a comfort zone mentality and to try to keep owners on their level.

Truthfully! really truthfully, Which One Are You? Because the only person who can seriously answer this question truthfully, is YOU.

☐ Comfort Zoner
☐ Owner

Tip: Stop giving people the power and authority to control and monitor your restroom breaks. Create your own freedom, it's possible. Let's Connect @KeithSmithOwner

CRITICS!

COMFORT ZONERS: Feed into critics advice. They curse critics out and get offended by what critics say about them or to them.

OWNERS: Do not tell critics off, but they smile critics off, ignore critics, and do not value critics opinions. They understand that critics are just spectators and not participators. Critics are stable in their comfort zone but not stable in growth.

Truthfully! really truthfully, Which One Are You? Because the only person who can seriously answer this question truthfully, is YOU.

☐ Comfort Zoner
☐ Owner

Tip: Stay productive and use critic's negative advice to push into your greatness, it's possible. Let's Connect @KeithSmithOwner

CRY!

COMFORT ZONERS: Try to cry stress off, financial debt off, bondage off, lack of ownership off and etc. They think that crying will change things.

OWNERS: They do not cry. They change their situation. They create a new way to be stress-free and financially free so they can get out of debt. They create a new way to get out of bondage. Owners do not cry their way out, they create their way out. They understand the power of joy through building and creating. Owners understand in order for things to change they have to be a part of and participate in their change. They understand the power of change starts with self-first.

Truthfully! really truthfully, Which One Are You? Because the only person who can seriously answer this question truthfully, is YOU.

☐ Comfort Zoner
☐ Owner

Tip: Stop crying and start participating in creating YOUR change, it's possible. Let's Connect @KeithSmithOwner

REJECT!

COMFORT ZONERS: Always feel neglected, rejected and want somebody to pity them, or to allow them to continue feeling bad about themselves..

OWNERS: Overcome the people that neglect and reject them.

Truthfully! really truthfully, Which One Are You? Because the only person who can seriously answer this question truthfully, is YOU.

☐ Comfort Zoner
☐ Owner

Tip: You were born to overcome obstacles, it's possible.
Let's Connect @KeithSmithOwner

HOW YOU DOING?

COMFORT ZONERS: Say things like this when you ask them how they are doing? "same stuff, different day". That is a sign of no growth talk, comfort zoners are scared to venture out on their own.

OWNERS: Say things like this when you ask them how they are doing? "Continuing moving upward and forward, always striving to improve and expand every day."

Truthfully! really truthfully, Which One Are You? Because the only person who can seriously answer this question truthfully, is YOU.

☐ Comfort Zoner
☐ Owner

Tip: You have the power to grow and expand. Use your power, it's possible. Let's Connect @KeithSmithOwner

ASK!

COMFORT ZONERS: When you ask them "how was your week or weekend?" They say, "great!" then you ask them, "what did you do?" they say, "nothing."

OWNERS: When you ask them "how was your week or weekend?" they say "great and productive!" Then you ask them, "what did you do?" They say, "well I was creating and expanding my vision." They give you breakdowns of how everything went.

Truthfully! really truthfully, Which One Are You? Because the only person who can seriously answer this question truthfully, is YOU.

☐ Comfort Zoner
☐ Owner

Tip: Give some explanations to the questions being asked by you, it's possible. Let's Connect @KeithSmithOwner

Destroy your Comfort Zone, or it will destroy you!

171 STRESS FREE!

COMFORT ZONERS: Say things like, "I am going to be stress-free" but they do nothing to become free.

OWNERS: Understand in order to become stress-free and to overcome circumstances they have to eliminate what is stressing them out or what is blocking their way to overcome their circumstances. They understand the power of elimination.

Truthfully! really truthfully, Which One Are You? Because the only person who can seriously answer this question truthfully, is YOU.

☐ Comfort Zoner
☐ Owner

Tip: Let go of unimportant things and people in your life right now to become more focus and productive, it's possible.
Let's Connect @KeithSmithOwner

172 GOSSIP!

COMFORT ZONERS: Are the people that just let anybody talk to them any type of way, persuade them to do anything, go anywhere people say go, do not think for themselves and wants everyone else to do their thinking for them, listen to people gossip and speak bad about other people. They eventually become negative, and start gossiping about other people. They spout what other people have told them.

OWNERS: They are the people that guard their ears because they understand if they listen to people that gossip and talk down about somebody else, it can eventually stop their growth and ability to create. Owners understand that the bible says, "take heed of what you hear and how you hear it". "Guard your heart because out of the heart issues of life flows". Owners understand the process of guarding what is valuable to them for it will not stop them from creating and expanding their vision that God has given them to create and expand with.

Truthfully! really truthfully, Which One Are You? Because the only person who can seriously answer this question truthfully, is YOU.

☐ Comfort Zoner
☐ Owner

Tip: Guard your ears and your heart from negativity, it's possible. Let's Connect @KeithSmithOwner

173 ENERGY!

COMFORT ZONERS: Are the people that are negative and full of envy. They have low energy, "sometimes no energy" and will try to deplete your energy. They are great at criticizing people.

OWNERS: Are the people that remain positive and uplifting. They have a lot of energy and want to share their positivity with other people. They create energy to give out. And most of all they are great at uplifting and encouraging Comfort Zoners to work for their company.

Truthfully! really truthfully, Which One Are You? Because the

Destroy your Comfort Zone, or it will destroy you!

only person who can seriously answer this question truthfully, is YOU.

☐ Comfort Zoner
☐ Owner

Tip: Do not let anyone take away your happiness and joyful energy, it's possible. Let's Connect @KeithSmithOwner

 # 174 DEBATES!

COMFORT ZONERS: Look for arguments, debates and fights.

OWNERS: Neglect and ignore arguments, debates and fights. They do not have time for things like that because their mind is on growth, creating and expanding.

Truthfully! really truthfully, Which One Are You? Because the only person who can seriously answer this question truthfully, is YOU.

☐ Comfort Zoner
☐ Owner

Tip: Ignore foolish things and foolish people, it's possible. Let's Connect @KeithSmithOwner

POINT!

COMFORT ZONERS: Yell and scream to try to get their point across.

OWNERS: Talk, communicate and get an understanding of the conversation they are having to get their point across.

Truthfully! really truthfully, Which One Are You? Because the only person who can seriously answer this question truthfully, is YOU.

☐ Comfort Zoner
☐ Owner

Tip: Become a great listener, so you can become an effective communicator. it's possible. Let's Connect @KeithSmithOwner

QUICK!

COMFORT ZONERS: Are quick to point out someone else's flaws.

OWNERS: Are quick to help people overcome their flaws.

Truthfully! really truthfully, Which One Are You? Because the only person who can seriously answer this question truthfully, is YOU.

☐ Comfort Zoner
☐ Owner

Destroy your Comfort Zone, or it will destroy you!

 # WORKING!

COMFORT ZONERS: Talk negative about the owner, say what the owner should be doing, say how much the owner should be paying them, say that the owner should be working.

OWNERS: They uplift the comfort zoner that work for them. If the owner works, they might just fire and replace the comfort zoner that is working and complaining about what the owner should be doing.

Truthfully! really truthfully, Which One Are You? Because the only person who can seriously answer this question truthfully, is YOU.

☐ Comfort Zoner
☐ Owner

 # UPLIFT!

COMFORT ZONERS: Only do things in life that make themselves feel good, uplift themselves and only to help themselves. In other words, they only invest in themselves and they simply spend time looking for what they can give themselves.

OWNERS: Do things in life that make other people feel good, uplift other people and help other people. They take the time to invest in everyone else before themselves and they look for what they can give others.

Truthfully! really truthfully, Which One Are You? Because the only person who can seriously answer this question truthfully, is YOU.

☐ Comfort Zoner
☐ Owner

> **Tip:** Invest in yourself, so you can be able to invest in someone else. It's possible. Let's Connect @KeithSmithOwner

INSIDE!

COMFORT ZONERS: Hold on to the love that is inside of them.

OWNERS: Give out and share the love they have inside of them with other people.

Truthfully! really truthfully, Which One Are You? Because the only person who can seriously answer this question truthfully, is YOU.

☐ Comfort Zoner
☐ Owner

> **Tip:** Share and spread some of your love around, it's possible. Let's Connect @KeithSmithOwner

Destroy your Comfort Zone, or it will destroy you!

CHILDREN!

COMFORT ZONERS: Are the people that have children and neglect them. They do not want to be bothered with their children and they stay away from their children.

OWNERS: Are the people that have children and take care of their responsibilities. They change their diaper, take them to school, help with their homework, support the events that they are a part of etc. They understand, if they laid down to have that child, they are responsible to get up and take care of that child.

Truthfully! really truthfully, Which One Are You? Because the only person who can seriously answer this question truthfully, is YOU.

☐ Comfort Zoner
☐ Owner

Tip: Love, cherish and take care of your children that you are bless to have, it's possible. Let's Connect @KeithSmithOwner

YEARS AGO!

COMFORT ZONERS: Talk about what happened to them ten years ago and still make no changes. They just like to be heard and do not want to be free. They like self-pity conversations and like to be around no growth people and relationships. They say things like, "my friends listen to me talk about what I have been going through and still going through for over ten years."

When a person continues to go through something for that long, you have become your own abuser, not the person or the thing you are blaming. Why are you still living in the past? Stop letting your future and present be your past, let go of your past so you can live in your future.

OWNERS: Talk about what they have accomplished and overcame from their past and what they are accomplishing now. Owners move forward and upward, they continuously keep growing and expanding their thoughts in their life. They do not let their past keep them down. They say things such as, "I have let go of my past, I am focused on my future, because my future is greater than my past as long as I continue to create and work towards it." Owner's say, "my past equals growth and my future equals expansion. I grow from my past and I expand in my future."

Truthfully! really truthfully, Which One Are You? Because the only person who can seriously answer this question truthfully, is YOU.

☐ Comfort Zoner
☐ Owner

Tip: Rise up and get past your past, it's possible. Let's Connect @KeithSmithOwner

182 THEMSELVES!

COMFORT ZONERS: Tear themselves down through negative words, thoughts, disbeliefs and guilt about themselves.

Destroy your Comfort Zone, or it will destroy you!

OWNERS: Build themselves up through positive words, thoughts, beliefs and confidence about themselves.

Truthfully! really truthfully, Which One Are You? Because the only person who can seriously answer this question truthfully, is YOU.

☐ Comfort Zoner
☐ Owner

Tip: Always encourage yourself, no matter how good or bad your circumstances may look, it's possible. Let's Connect @KeithSmithOwner

 # 183 HURT!

COMFORT ZONERS: Say and think people are always trying to hurt them. They say things like, "you are not trying to help me, you are trying to hurt me. It does not take all of this pain for growth, you want to see me fail."

OWNERS: Understand growth and expansion comes along with some hurt and pain. It allows them to stretch and move forward. They understand it is not there to hurt them but it is there to help them. It is called life.

Truthfully! really truthfully, Which One Are You? Because the only person who can seriously answer this question truthfully, is YOU.

☐ Comfort Zoner
☐ Owner

I BECAME....

SHORT STORY!

There's this hard working man named Tony, who is a Real estate agent and married with two beautiful children. Every day Tony gets off work, and takes the same route home. As he approaches this one corner he always catches a red light, he notices a gentleman, Bob. Bob always stands there with his cup out, begging for change every day. Tony lets his window down and gives Bob money every day he sees him, six days out of the week.

One day Tony decided to park his car and ask the beggar for his name.

He replied "My name is Bob, and what is yours if you don't mind me asking you sir?"

Tony said "You don't have to call me sir, but my name is Tony".

Bob said, "Nice to meet you Tony, and thank you so much for always helping a homeless man out every time you see me".

Tony said "No problem, that is my job and passion to give to homeless people that are in need every time I see them. I just believe that is the right thing to do because we all have hard times. That's why I always give every time I see you Bob."

With appreciation, Bob replied,"Thank you Tony, for having such a compassionate heart for people like me".

Tony said "You're welcome, Bob. I have to get going, but I just wanted to get your name and talk to you for a little while. God bless you Bob and I hope your situation gets better."

Bob said "Thank you Tony, and God bless you as well".

As Tony was driving off along came another gentleman named Jim. Jim was a business owner of a very profitable organization. Tony and Jim always took the same route home. Just like Tony, Jim sees Bob standing at the corner with his cup out begging for money every day. Jim gets caught at the stop light as well. Bob approaches his vehicle with his cup out, shaking his cup and begging for money.

Jim let his window down and asked the beggar "What is your name?"

The beggar said "my name is Bob and if you don't mind me asking you. What is your name sir?"

Jim said, "You don't have to call me sir but my name is Jim".

Bob said, "It's a pleasure to meet you Jim".

Jim nodded, "Likewise, Bob.. I'm going to park my car so I can get out and talk to you. So we won't hold up traffic."

Bob said "That's fine".

As Jim got out of his car and approached Bob, he asked him, "What got you to this place?"

Bob instantly drops his head and tears start pouring out of his eyes. He said while sobbing and stuttering, "Jim it's hard for me to talk about how I got here. I choose not to talk about it because it brings back so many harsh memories."

PART 5: EMOTIONALLY

Jim looked at Bob and said "Bob hold your head up, because I have something to tell you and I want you to hear what I'm about to tell you loud and clear."

Bob lifts his head up and slowly wiping the tears from his eyes and said "I'm listening, sir". As Jim looked Bob in his eyes, he said "Bob listen to me, if you are lying about being homeless just to get money out of people, you are going to really become homeless no matter how much money you deceive people out of, because you are SPEAKING those homeless words over your life every day. Words are very powerful Bob because they are what shapes your life and future daily. So just to let you know, whenever you see me from this time on, I would like for you to know this about me. I do not just give homeless people money or materialistic things, but I do offer to teach them how to get their own money or materialistic things if they choose to accept my offering. So with that being said Bob, would you like a job?"

Bob looked at Jim and said, "No, thanks. I will just continue to wait on this same corner at this same stop light for the ones who will give to me because they have compassion for people like me."

Jim looked at Bob and said "Have a great day Bob but just remember if you would like a job the offer is here for you".

Bob said, "thanks Jim, and have a great day as well."

The next day Tony saw Bob standing at the same corner. Tony said, "Hey there, Bob! How are you doing today?"

Bob said, "I'm taking it day by day, Tony. I really thank God for compassionate people like you Tony, after talking to an uncompassionate guy name Jim yesterday. By the way, do you know a Jim, Tony?"

Tony said, "Not that I can think of. No I don't think I have known a Jim in my life."

Bob said, "Good, I hope you never run into that selfish guy. My God, is he selfish."

Tony said "Well, I just wanted to stop by. Because I knew that you would be out here. So I had my wife to make you a meal and here goes $10 for you as well, Bob".

Bob said "Thank you, Tony."

"You're Welcome, Bob." Tony replied, "God bless you and I hope your situation gets better."

Bob said "I hope so too, Tony."

So Tony was giving money to Bob on his way home every day for three years straight. He started giving Bob half of his rent money because the more he saw Bob on that corner the more he became more compassionate towards Bob's situation. Tony's wife began to question him about the finances and where they were going because they started getting behind on their mortgage.

Tony said, "Baby, I'm helping a homeless man to do better in his life. I feel if we help the homeless we will not lose anything".

The more Tony was helping Bob, the more Tony's wife was becoming more frustrated because they were getting behind in all of their bills. His wife left him because they lost their house, their vehicle and Tony lost his job. Tony became so stressed that he didn't know what to do because he lost everything while trying to help the homeless man. So one day Tony decided to walk where he knew Bob would be.

Tony stood on the same corner that Bob used to stand on and started holding out a cup begging for change while full of hurt and tears in his eyes. Tony couldn't find him. Bob was nowhere to be found, day after day.

Two years passed, and Tony stood on that street corner every day, begging as Bob once did. One day as Tony was in Bob spot begging for change. A Lamborghini ($200,000 car) pulled up to the stop light where Tony was standing.

Tony runs to the car window and says, "Sir, can you please help me? I really need your help."

The gentleman cracks his window and says, "Thank you so much Tony for helping me to become rich. I was never homeless, that was my job duty to stand in that spot where you are standing at right now to scam heartfelt compassionate people like you out of your money. I hope your situation gets better. God bless you, and one thing about me Tony I do not give money to homeless people. So figure out how you are going to make it out here".

As Bob pulled off in his Lamborghini, Tony fell to his knees in disbelief with full of tears running down his cheeks and said to himself silently. "WOW! I became the man that i thought I was helping and lost everything, including my family". While kneeling in the same spot where Bob used to be standing at begging for money. Tony cries out to the Lord and says "Lord please help me to get my family back. I really need my family back."

As Jim took a different route home while driving a different vehicle, he saw Bob again. Bob came up to his car shaking his cup.

Jim let his window down and Bob said "Sir, do you have some money to help me?"

Jim said, "Hey there, Bob I see you move from your last location that you used to stand at".

Bob said, "Oh hey there Jim. I didn't recognize you because of this different car you in from the last time I spoke with you".

Destroy your Comfort Zone, or it will destroy you!

Jim then asked Bob, "Why did you move from your last location?"

Bob instantly drops his head and tears instantly start pouring from his eyes again like the first time Jim asked him a question. He said while sobbing and stuttering. "Jim it's hard for me to talk about why I change locations. I choose not to talk about it because it bring back so many harsh memories".

Jim looked at Bob and said "Bob, hold your head up because I have something to tell you and I want you to hear what I'm about to tell you loud and clear".

Bob lifts his head up and slowly wiping the tears from his eyes and said "I'm listening sir."

As Jim looked Bob in his eyes he said "Bob listen to me. Like I said the last time I spoke with you, if you are lying about being homeless just to get money out of people, you are going to really become homeless no matter how much money you deceive people out of because you are SPEAKING those homeless words over your life every day. Words are very powerful because they are what shapes your life and future daily. So Bob just to let you know, whenever you see me from this time on. I would like for you to know this about me. I do not just give homeless people money or materialistic things but I do offer to teach them how to get their own money or materialistic things if they choose to accept my offering. So with that being said Bob. Would you like a job?"

Bob looked at Jim for the second offer and said, "No thanks, Jim. I will just continue to wait on this same corner at this same stop light for the ones who will give to me because they have compassion for people like me."

Jim looked at Bob and said, "Have a great day Bob, but just remember if you would like a job the offer is here for you"

PART 5: EMOTIONALLY

Bob said, "Thanks Jim, and have a great day".

As Jim was driving off he decided instead of just going straight home he drives past the corner Bob used to stand at. Tony comes up to his car shaking his cup and begging for change.

"Sir can you please help me, please help me, I really need your help sir".

Jim said, "Ok let me park so I can get out and talk to you".

As Jim approached Tony he asked him, "What is your name?"

He said, "My name is Tony, sir and I really need help, I really need help".

Jim said, "Tony you can call me Jim you don't have to call me sir. But you seems to really be in desperate need for help out of a lot of homeless people I talk to. I understand you need help Tony and that you are homeless. But if you don't mind can you share with me a little background about yourself and how you got here?"

Tony said sure. "I was a very successful real estate agent with a wife and two beautiful children. I had a happy home and was married for 25 years before my wife left me with my two beautiful daughters".

Jim interrupted Tony and asked "Why did she leave you?"

Tony instantly fell to his knees and start sobbing and put his head down. Jim instantly thought to himself, "oh here goes another Bob story."

Jim asked, "Tony are you going to be able to carry on with the story or is it too hard to talk about it because it bring back harsh memories?" Tony said "Jim, just give me one moment please because it's harsh to talk about it but I have to talk about it because

I really need help". Tony then lifted up his head to tell his story. He said "Jim when I was a real estate agent, I used to get off work and ride past this place that we are standing at right now every day. So one day a guy approached my car the same way that I approached yours, as I looked at him I felt sorry and compassionate for him. I began to give him money every day for three years straight and had my wife to cook him food. Jim interrupts, "Three years straight, Tony?"

Tony drops his head again while sobbing and stuttering, "Yes three years straight Jim. I gave so much to this guy I began to start being late on paying my mortgage. Jim, not only that but the last time I gave to him my wife left me because I lost the house, our vehicle and my job". As Tony was talking, Jim began to tear up because he realized this guy really does need help. "As I lost everything I decided to come back to this location where we are standing at right now because I wanted to know the gentleman's story about how he ended up standing here begging for change like I am right now. But as I approached this place he was nowhere to be found. So I decided to stay out here every day to beg for help and hoping he will show up to tell me his story about how he became homeless and lost everything he had."

One day as I was standing out here going car to car begging for change a Lamborghini pulled up to this same stop light where we are at. I ran to the car window like I did yours, Jim with my cup in my hand and said "Sir can you please help me? I really need your help." The gentleman cracked his window and said "Thank you so much, Tony, for helping me to become rich. I was NEVER homeless that was my job duty to stand in that spot where you are standing at right now to scam heartfelt compassionate people like you out of your money. I hope your situation gets better. God bless you and one thing about me Tony I do not give money to homeless people. So figure out how you are going to make it out here." As he pulled off in his Lamborghini, I fell to my knees in disbelief

PART 5: EMOTIONALLY

with full of tears running down my cheeks and said to myself silently. "WOW! I became the man that I thought I was helping and lost everything I had including my family." Then I cried out to God to help me. I said "Lord please help me to get my family back. I need your help."

Jim wiping his eyes from crying after listening to Tony's heartfelt story and said, "Tony I do not know who you are, but you have greatness inside of you. It is a guy who used to stand here and beg for money just like you are doing. I told him something and I'm going to tell you the same thing that I told him even though your story is compelling, compassionate and heartfelt.

"But Tony I have something to tell you and I want you to hear what I'm about to tell you loud and clear. Tony, listen to me. If you are lying about being homeless just to get money out of people. You are going to really become homeless no matter how much money you deceive people out of because you are SPEAKING those homeless words over your life every day. Tony words are very powerful because they is what shapes your life and future daily. So just to let you know whenever you see me from this time on. I would like for you to know this about me. I do not just give homeless people money or materialistic things but I do offer to teach them how to get their own money or materialistic things if they choose to accept my offering. So with that being said, Tony. Would you like a job?"

Tony immediately said "Yes".

Jim said "With your story and your work history I would like to make you one of the supervisors in my company. Now get in this car so we can go and get you cleaned up and so you can get back to work and get your family back."

Tony asked with tears running down his cheeks, "How am I'm going to find my family?"

Jim said, "Don't worry about that because I have a friend that owns a business where they specialize in finding love ones for others".

Tony said "Wow Jim! with a big smile on his face, you are going to help me get my family back and a job? That's all I've ever wanted back was my family. Thank you, Jim."

Jim said "No Tony you are helping yourself to get a job and your family back because you chose to accept my offer presented to you. So I want to say THANK you, Tony. By the way Tony, who is the guy you used to give money to and your wife cooked meals for that was portraying himself to be homeless?

"His name was Bob, Jim."

Jim echoes, "BOB?, Tony did you just say "BOB?"

"Yeah I said "bob". So do you know him Jim?"

"Don't worry about that Tony."

"Wait one minute," Tony said out loud. "You are the Jim that Bob was saying is selfish and uncompassionate. Wow, I am pleased to meet you."

Jim had a small talk with Tony before they drove off in the car.

"Hey Tony?"

"Yeah Jim?" Tony replied.

"Listen to me loud and clear Tony, never be deceived again. Always ask people to tell you their story to how they ended up in their situation in the first place. Because if they are bold enough to ask you for something you should be bold enough to ask them a question that you would like to know before giving them something if you choose to give them something. Then if their story is compelling and compassionate to you, offer to teach them how to make money and never just give them money. There are many people portraying to be homeless and people just give them money and materialistic things like you were doing for Bob instead of teaching him how to make money. Tony, a lot of people think that they are doing the will of God when they just give homeless people a one-time financial fee instead of giving them a lifetime investment of knowledge. Rather it's giving them a job or giving them advice about how to get a job or create a job for themselves. When the bible clearly says that the wealth of the wicked is stored up for the Righteous. Not the wealth of the righteous is stored up for the wicked. The wicked are deceiving the righteous people by portraying themselves to be homeless or in need. So Tony always make sure you get a Godly understanding on who to give to or you will always become homeless just giving out of your sympathy and emotions for them". Do you understand what I just said to you Tony?

"Yes Jim," Tony replied.

"Alright come on, let's get going now."

As time went on Bob really lost everything and as he was standing on corners begging for change and food, there wasn't anyone giving him anything. He became so frustrated with himself, his body became abated, he had run down shoes, he was sleeping under cardboard boxes, under bridges, eating out of garbage cans every day, had the same clothes on day and night, sleeping on trains and his clothes was smelling so bad that whenever he walked past people they instantly covered their noses and quickly tried to move out of his way. He was banned from every store he tried to go in or that he tried to stand in front of to beg for change that he really needed. People even banned Bob from eating out of their garbage cans. Bob was so hungry from day to day that he would kill cats just to skin some meat off of them to eat. One day Bob decided to go stand back in the same spot where he was at when

Tony used to give him money.

But the people that used to give to Bob began to look at him and keep their windows rolled up as he approach their car with his same cup in his hand while shaking, limping, sobbing, stuttering, smelling and really hungry and begging for money just to get a bag of chips or a bottle of water to put in his stomach for that day. No one gave to him for one year straight. So one day while standing in that same spot where he mislead thousands of people by portraying to be homeless. Bob said to himself silently and in desperate need. "WOW! I really became the homeless man who I was portraying to be".

While reflecting on the words that Jim told him every time he saw him. Jim was right when he told me, "that words were powerful and that I was speaking and shaping my life and future everyday by portraying and telling people that I was homeless just to get money out of them". Meanwhile, while I was thinking I'm fooling and deceiving other people. I BECAME THE REAL FOOL. Bob then looked up to the sky and said "LORD I need your help, please get me out of this homeless pit. Forgive me Lord for deceiving so many people. I NEED HELP!"

Jim runs into Bob again and said "Bob you still out here, huh?"

Bob said "Yeah Jim, I'm really out here now."

Jim said "Bob trust me I really don't want to know your story any more after hearing Tony's story".

Bob said "WAIT! How do you know Tony?"

Jim said "Trust me Bob, I rather not talk about Tony with you. But my last and final question to you Bob is would you like a job?"

Bob looked down at his clothes and start crying instantly. Jim said to himself "Here he goes with this sad harsh memory story again".

Bob looked up at Jim, "Jim! I will take the job".

Jim said to Bob "What took you so long to accept a job?"

Bob said "I choose not to talk about it yet Jim".

Then Bob said "Jim if you don't mind me asking you. Can you tell me a little history about yourself?"

Jim said "Of course, thanks for asking me that most imperative question".

Jim said, "See Bob, when I was younger I used to be a person that loved to just give money to any homeless person I saw because I had a successful job with a wife and two beautiful daughters and I felt that was the right thing to do. So this one guy I used to give money to every week for two years straight decided that he wanted to let me know the truth about himself. His name was Billy".

Bob interrupts Jim and said "WAIT! I think I know a Billy. I know I lost some of my memory but the Billy I know became homeless after some years of having millions of dollars. If this is the same Billy you're talking about, Jim he was my friend. But continue on with your story Jim."

"So like I was saying, Bob. Billy started telling me that this was his day time job to act like he is homeless so he can get money out of people. He said that he makes over $200,000 a year portraying to be something that he's not. After Billy told me that. I was captured by his story and very intrigued about how much he profited every year. So as time went on I became like him".

Bob said "Like who? Like Billy?"

Jim said "Yeah like Billy. I started to act as though I was homeless for about three years Bob. As I was on the corner begging for change this gentleman let down his window and said those exact words I told you when I first met you. He said to me bob "Jim I will not give you money but I will teach you how to make money. Then he said young man if you are not really homeless and you are portraying to be homeless you are going to eventually become what you are portraying to be because words are powerful and they shape your life and future daily. So one day I silently said to myself in tears WOW! I became the man that I was portraying to be which was homeless. I then looked up to the sky said "Lord forgive me for hurting and misleading thousands of people by portraying to be something that I wasn't which was homeless just to gain more money. Bob, I kept saying to myself Billy was right my words that I was speaking over my life everyday has really shaped my life and future that I really became a homeless man. But that guy that helped me to get a job and to get back on my feet was the same man that went through everything I went through. He was Billy. That's why he was able to ride by the stop light that I was at and tell me those life investment words."

Bob said "wait, is that why you don't give money out to people because you don't know who is really homeless and who are portraying to be homeless but you offer them a job and a lifetime investment of powerful words?"

Jim said "that is exactly why I do that because I've been through it. Not only have I been through it but Billy been through it and you are just now coming out of it Bob. Bob said "Wait! I never told you my story, how do you know that?" Jim said "you didn't have to tell me your story. because the guy Tony that became homeless by helping you to become rich because you were portraying to be homeless has told me your story". But let's leave this conversation alone and move forward now. Bob from this point on, like Billy always teaches me and I want to share this lifetime of knowledge with you. Are you listening Bob? "Jim asked.

"Yes I'm listening." Bob replied.

PART 5: EMOTIONALLY

Jim said "NEVER give homeless people money or materialistic things but give them a choice and a offer on how to make money. Because if you keep giving them money Bob, you will always have to give them money when you see them like Tony was doing with you. So you are not helping them to come out of their situation by giving them money. You are actually helping them to stay in their situation and helping them to stay crippled and in bondage by giving them money and materialistic things. But when you offer to give them a job or teach them how to make money for themselves, you know longer will see them on that corner begging for change anymore. So Bob, instead of you investing in them for that moment by giving them money, you have just invested in them by giving them a job to make their own money and they don't have to stand on the corner anymore with a cup in their hand begging for change".

"WOW! Jim I really like that advice". Bob replied.

"So Jim, what if I offer them a job and they don't want the job or they don't want me to teach them how to make money for themselves what do I do then?" Should I just give them the money?"

Jim said "No ABSOLUTELY NOT. Like I said before Bob, NEVER give them the money no matter what their story is or how compassionate you feel about them after hearing their story. Hey Bob, do you remember when I offered you a job after talking to you?"

"Yeah" bob responded.

"What was your first and second answer after I offered you a job?"

Bob said "I said I will just stand out here and beg and wait for the compassionate heartfelt people to come".

"Did I give you money after you said no to my job offering, Bob?"

"No." Bob replied.

"What did I do after you refused my job offer?"

Bob said, "You said the job offer is still available when I'm ready and then you drove off."

"Do you know why I drove off after you refused my job offer?"

"Yes, because you used to portray yourself as a homeless person, so you understood the scam".

Jim responded, "no, that is not the exact reason but that is part of the reason". The exact reason that I did not give you money and I drove off, is because I've learned that people in this world whether they are homeless or not don't really want help, they want a handout. They want everything given to them instead of going and working for what they need. So people that tell me that they want my money instead of my advice to help them generate more money for themselves, I tell them "that I will see them soon but I NEVER go into my pocket to give them money". Like I said "I will always be going in my pocket to give them money like Tony did with you every time I see them because they don't want help they want handouts."

"So Bob, from now on never give handouts but always offer a way of help to them. Like I said earlier "only offer people a lifetime of knowledge that you can invest in them". Also let them know if they are out here portraying to be homeless just to get money out of people by deceiving them. They will become homeless because their words that they are speaking over their life every day is shaping their life and future daily to what they will really become. You never know who is out here portraying to be homeless like we were doing. Now come on knucklehead and get in this car so we can go get you cleaned up and working like a real man is supposed to."

Bob looked at Jim with a smirk on his face and said "A real man ,huh?"

Jim responded back quickly and said "As I said "LIKE A REAL MAN IS SUPPOSED TO."

Truthfully! really truthfully, Which One Are You? Because the only person who can seriously answer this question truthfully, is YOU.

☐ Tony- who just gives money to homeless people because you feel that's the right thing to do.

☐ Bob- Who portray to be homeless.

☐ Jim- Who offers lifetime investment to the homeless people through words or helping them Get a job.

Tip: You played the role to become homeless. Now you have play the role to become free from being homeless. You have the power to break any bad habits. So stop blaming others for your downfalls and feeling self-pity for yourself. Nobody owes you anything. Always remember this, nobody or nothing stop you from achieving anything in your life but you. IT'S POSSIBLE!
Let's Connect @KeithSmithOwner

185 YES/NO!

When people say "YES" to your Service or Product that you offer them. Let that Inspire you to be GRATEFUL.

When people say "NO" to your Service or Product that you offer them. Let that Inspire you to keep going unto you get a YES.

But whether people say YES or NO to your Service or Product. Let that Inspire you to be THANKFUL. Because they took the time out of their schedule to listen to you present your service or product to them.

> **Tip:** Can't nobody stop you but you, it's possible.
> Let's Connect @KeithSmithOwner

186 YOUR VISION!

Your vision that's inside of you have the capability to impact millions of people LIVES. But if you give up on your vision because of critics, obstacles and rejections that comes to stop you then your Vision DIES.

> **Tip:** Don't give anyone or anything the power to make you give up on your vision. Continue working your vision. Stay committed, focused and ambitious. Keep the faith so you can see your vision grow and expand. IT'S POSSIBLE!
> Let's Connect @KeithSmithOwner

187 STOP EXPECTING PEOPLE TO!

1. Believe in your Vision, if you don't even Believe in Your own Vision.

2. Trust You if DON'T even trust yourself.

3. Forgive you for what you have done if you don't even forgive others or yourself for what you have done.

4. Be on time for your event if you not even on time for you Own Event or Someone else's Event.

5. Follow you if don't even know what DIRECTION you are going in.

6. Make you happy if you don't even know how to make yourself happy.

7. Respect you if you don't even respect yourself.

8. Care for you if you don't even care for yourself.

9. Love you if you don't even love yourself.

10. Listen to what you are saying if you are always interrupting others as they are talking.

11. Tell you the Truth if you are always lying to others and YOURSELF.

Destroy your Comfort Zone, or it will destroy you!

12. Be Faithful to you if you are always cheating on YOU by cheating on them.

☆The Bottom line is STOP Blaming People for YOUR Mistakes, Peace, Joy, Happiness, Failures and Direction for your Life and Take Ownership for Every Breathing Area of Your Own Life. It's Possible.

"ACKNOWLEDGE YOUR COMFORT ZONE and DESTROY IT daily to become a Better YOU" It's Possible!

My Reflection Notes

Write down the topic number(s) that you TRUTHFULLY know
that you need to improve in and why?

SPECIAL THANKS to #32!

#32- Represents my age when I first started writing this book "Comfort Zoners vs Owners-Truthfully, Which One Are You?

ACKNOWLEDGEMENT and INSPIRING THANKS TO:

My Lord and Savior: JESUS CHRIST

My faithful, Uplifting and Encouraging Wife: Lilreka Smith

My Daughters: Kaleah and Promise Smith. Daddy Love Yall.

My Mom's: Gloria Smith and Lillian Williams.

Gloria Smith- who has raised eleven of my brothers and sisters by herself in one home since my twin brother Kyle Smith (Author of "Questions We All Have Regarding") and I were one year old. Who has always been a giver and fed others children as well, while never neglecting to feed her own. Who will rub your feet and scratch your back even while her feet are hurting and her back is itching.

True story: When my mom Gloria Smith was in the hospital on bed rest after having surgery. One of my Uncles came in to visit her. As they were talking, my Uncle told my mom how his foot was hurting him, she told him to take his shoe and socks off and put his foot on her hospital bed, so she can rub them because she did not want to see him in pain while she was in pain. He then took his shoes and socks off and put his feet on the hospital bed. My mom began rubbing his feet. As she was rubbing his feet he said to her, it feels better now. She looked at him and said, "now I can get some rest, since I know that you're not in pain anymore." She then turned over and went to bed.

Lillian Williams- Who has treated me not as a son-in-law but as her son. Who always has a dinner ready for me whenever my wife and I come over to her house. Who is a giver and feeds her neighbors before she feeds herself. Who never misses a Sunday for church and I mean never.

My Father: Ronald Smith (Rip)

My Siblings: Love you all.

Editors: Heidy De La Cruz, Tiana Ashley

Book Consultant: ARD Book Services

AUTHOR CONTACT INFORMATION
Contact Keith Smith for speaking engagements, motivational speaking, and seminars.

P.O. Box 1792
Bridgeview, IL 60455
Email: keithsmithowner@gmail.com

This book is online at www.amazon.com

To make a payment or if you would like to give a donation, it will be greatly appreciated. Please feel free to:

Cash App $KeithSmithOwner

QuickPay or Zelle @ keithsmithowner@gmail.com

I THANK YOU IN ADVANCE FOR YOUR SUPPORT!!!

Destroy your Comfort Zone, or it will destroy you!

COMFORT ZONERS
-VS-
OWNERS

Truthfully, Which One Are You?

To make a payment or if you would like to give a donation, it will be greatly appreciated. Please feel free to:

Cash App $KeithSmithOwner

QuickPay or Zelle @ keithsmithowner@gmail.com

I THANK YOU IN ADVANCE FOR YOUR SUPPORT!!!

Destroy your Comfort Zone, or it will destroy you!